M000309598

Galley Slave

GALLEY SLAVE

Jean Marteilhe

*Edited with an introduction by
Vincent McInerney*

Seaforth
PUBLISHING

This edition copyright © Vincent McInerney 2010

First published in Great Britain in 2010 by
Seaforth Publishing,
Pen & Sword Books Ltd,
47 Church Street,
Barnsley S70 2AS

www.seaforthpublishing.com

British Library Cataloguing in Publication Data

A catalogue record for this book is available
from the British Library

ISBN 978 1 84832 070 3

Typeset and designed by M.A.T.S. Leigh-on-Sea, Essex
Printed and bound in Great Britain by Cromwell Press Group

Contents

Editorial note   ix
Introduction   1

Galley Slave
Foreword: A description of a galley,
  its crew, and method of fighting   33

1 Flight and capture 1700-1701   39
2 The prisons at Tournay and Lille   56
3 To Dunkirk in the galley chain 1702   73
4 Incidents at the galleys, Dunkirk 1703-1705   89
5 We almost perish in a great storm,
   Dunkirk 1707   95
6 Our galley destroyed, the crew
   massacred, Dunkirk 1708   103
7 At Dunkirk 1709   119
8 We are removed with great torments from the
   galleys at Dunkirk to those at Marseilles 1712   132
9 The last of the chains 1713   178

Notes   207

Editorial Note

> He who was captured . . . was set to row until he died.
> And the calculating mercy which causes a man to
> feed and treat his beast well in order that it might do
> better work was not to be relied on here; as life was
> cheap and slaves were plentiful.[1]

> *The Memoirs of a Protestant Condemned to the
> Galleys of France for his Religion*. Written by
> Himself. In two volumes. Translated from the
> Original just published at the Hague, by JAMES
> WILLINGTON. London, 1758.

THE ABOVE ADVERTISEMENT was for what is usually
considered to be the first, 1758, English translation of
the autobiography of Jean Marteilhe (1684-1777).
Marteilhe was a French Protestant Huguenot condemned to the Mediterranean galleys from 1701-1713 for
his religion. His *Memoirs* present a compelling and
unique account unlike any other in the annals of
autobiographical maritime history.

The translator's name, James Willington, is a
pseudonym for Oliver Goldsmith (1730-1774), James

Willington having been a fellow pupil of Goldsmith's at Trinity College, Dublin. It was thought Goldsmith may have come across the book on a continental walking tour: he was in Leiden, Holland, in 1754, and Holland was Marteilhe's base. Goldsmith returned to England in February 1756 and two years later the *Memoirs* were published. As the *Cambridge History of English and American Literature* (1907-1921) states, Goldsmith 'may, indeed, have actually seen Marteilhe in Holland; but it is more reasonable to suppose that he was attracted to the subject by the advertisement, in *The Monthly Review* for May, 1757, of the French original.'[2]

The French original was an edition published anonymously as *Mémoires d'un Protestant Condamné aux Galères de France*, etc, by J. D. Beman at Rotterdam in 1757. The actual source for this first edition seems itself shrouded in mystery. By using the French text advertised in the *Monthly Review*, Goldsmith would have had nine months to negotiate the translation, deliver the manuscript for the agreed £20 fee (he sold the rights to three investors, receiving £6 13s 4d from each) and for the book to be on the shelves by February 1758. The alternative would have been to use an earlier edition which Goldsmith may have seen, or possibly acquired in Holland. There was a further Rotterdam edition edited by Daniel de Superville sometime after 1757; a Dublin edition, printed for E.

Watts in 1765; two Hague editions were published in 1774 and 1778 before the *Memoirs* were issued as part of Goldsmith's *Miscellaneous Works* by John Murray, London, 1837. A Paris edition of 1864 edited by Henry Paumier was followed by the Religious Tract Society's edition, *c.*1880, and an 1895 Dent, London and Mead, New York edition. There was an edition illustrated with contemporary seventeenth- and eighteenth-century prints issued by Louis-Michaud, Paris in 1909.

The following edited abridgement for the Seafarers' Voices series is taken from the text of the 1765 Dublin edition, which contains some afternotes by Marteilhe, important for the introduction that follows this editorial note, plus that of the Religious Tract Society, both on certain points being referenced back to the Rotterdam first edition. The word count has been reduced roughly by half, from 80,000 to 40,000. The lost material relates primarily to seventeenth-century theological and political issues of limited interest to the modern reader, and to some that took place almost entirely onshore, some hearsay. Spelling and punctuation and the use of capitalised nouns have been modernised.

Goldsmith may have been attracted to Marteilhe for a number of reasons. The book is a good read: 'An exceedingly free and racy version of one of the most authentic records of the miseries ensuing on the revocation of the Edict of Nantes.'[1] Goldsmith, in debt throughout his life, may also have seen such an enthralling and unusual work as representing a sound commercial venture.

Marteilhe's reasons for writing were very different. His primary task was to expose the 'miseries' to which his fellow religionists were subjected on being sentenced to serve as slaves on the French Mediterranean galleys. These miseries and servitude were brought about, as he perceived it, by the cruelties and inhumanities of the Catholic church, and which stemmed, at their most oppressive, from the revocation of the above-mentioned Edict of Nantes.

Introduction

THE VALUE TO THE contemporary reader of Jean
Marteilhe's account of the trials and tribulations of his
life as a galley slave in the early eighteenth century lies
not only in the fact that he writes an exciting tale of
misadventure, violence and intrigue, but also in the
uniqueness of his memoir as historical record. As
Fenwick pointed out in 1957, this 'is the only full-length
account of the life of the galley slave and it contains
information unavailable elsewhere.'[3] Marteilhe's
distinctive voice and compelling tale provides a fitting
introduction to this series of memoirs of seafarers from
the past.

Jean Marteilhe's descriptions of his life as a prisoner
of conscience aboard the French galleys are set at a time
of religious and political strife, when the nations of
Europe were regularly at war with each other, and the
importance of sea power was increasing significantly.
Marteilhe was a French Protestant, a Huguenot, and
one of a class of people persecuted by church and state
in France for their faith. By his account he was
unwilling to compromise his principles for the sake of

expediency and freedom, and writes vividly of the
gruelling experiences he suffered as a galley slave in
consequence. His compelling memoirs take us back to
early eighteenth-century France and the internecine sea
battles between European powers, as well as the violent
and often cruel treatment meted out to prisoners of all
kinds. Marteilhe was a prisoner both on land and on
sea, and his colourful account of the vicissitudes of life
aboard the galleys, prison ships manned by slaves, and
commanded by aristocrats in search of a sinecure,
locates his experience firmly in the contemporary
politics and society of eighteenth-century Europe.

Although Marteilhe's memoirs are set in the early years
of the eighteenth century, the history of Protestantism in
France began two centuries before, a history of religious
unrest and religiously-motivated violence, stretching
back to the early sixteenth century when the first
national Protestant church of France was born. France,
essentially a Catholic country, began to see these
Protestants, designated in France as Huguenots, and
their religion as a threat for, although the Huguenots
comprised only a small fraction of the French
population, their wealth and influence began to cause
envy, anger and resentment. Eight French wars
of religion (1562-1598) followed, including the St
Bartholomew's Day massacre of 1572, which took place
shortly after the wedding of the Protestant Henry III of

Navarre to the Catholic Marguerite de Valois; this Paris-based massacre presaged thousands of Huguenots losing their lives in the following months as the killings spread throughout France.

By 1590, Protestant Henry III of Navarre was now Protestant Henry IV of France and, realising that the Parisians would never accept a Protestant king, Henry is said to have uttered the famous remark that 'Paris is well worth a mass', and converted to Catholicism in 1593, before being officially crowned at Chartres in 1594. In an attempt to stabilise the country, promote civil unity, and project toleration towards his old co-religionists, Henry in 1598 promulgated the Edict of Nantes. This guaranteed Henry's Protestant (Huguenot) subjects liberty of conscience and worship, absolute security of person and property, and equal rights and privileges before the law. This Edict continued in force for nearly ninety years, 'although its stipulations were often violated under one pretence or another.'[4]

In October 1685, the Edict was revoked by Louis XIV, and Huguenot clergy were commanded to leave the kingdom within fifteen days under pain of being condemned to the galleys. All Protestant worship was banned and many churches razed to the ground; all Protestant schools were to be closed and all children born after the date of the Revocation were to be baptised and brought up as Catholics. Adults who had been born and raised as Protestants were expected to remain in the country 'until it shall please God to enlighten them.' Any caught attempting to escape from the kingdom would be sentenced to the galleys.

The English diarist John Evelyn wrote on 3 November 1685 that '[t]he French persecution of the Protestants raging with the utmost barbarity, exceeded even what the very heathens used. Innumerable persons of the greatest birth and riches leaving all their earthly substance and hardly escaping with their lives, dispersed through all the countries of Europe.'[5] Every effort was made by Louis' dragoons to close the frontiers, but many Huguenots did reach England, Switzerland, Holland, or Germany: the final figure was put at about two hundred thousand.

Notwithstanding the large number who escaped France, within a year of the Revocation there were more than six hundred Huguenots in the galleys at Marseilles, as many at Toulon, and a proportionate number at other ports. Initially, upon capture, the slaves would be shackled together in what were termed 'galley chains', and then:

> On all the roads of the kingdom, these miserable wretches might be seen, burdened by heavy chains . . . Sometimes sinking to the ground with exhaustion, but being compelled to rise by blows from the guards. Their food unwholesome, and insufficient – for the guards pocketed half the amount allowed. At night lodged in foul dungeons, or barns where they lay

upon the bare earth, without covering, weighed down by their chains.[6]

Jean Marteilhe was one of these who eventually marched in a chain, and it is his account that gives us the rare eyewitness account we have of the day-to-day life in the French Mediterranean galleys, written from the point of view of a slave.

The galley has a long history. Primarily a Mediterranean fighting vessel, its main propulsion came from human oarsmen, although masts and sails were often employed, and its short bursts of speed made it a potent weapon for catching and ramming enemy ships. Although of various dimensions, the galleys in which Marteilhe served were 'ordinarily a hundred and fifty feet long, and forty feet broad': that is, approximately five London red buses in length by one and a third in width; their depth, mid-deck to keel was about seven feet.

Galleys have been known since the Old Kingdom in Egypt, between two and three thousand years before the birth of Christ, at the time of the building of the pyramids. This places the origin of the galley firmly in the Mediterranean. Viking ships were, of course, a type of galley, active in the Baltic Sea and further afield (and later in the eighteenth century Sweden and Russia employed them in their wars, when their handling characteristics made them useful in confined waters), but the Mediterranean has always been seen as the spiritual home of the galley. Unlike the clinker-built Viking ship, the Mediterranean galley was carvel-built, that is, with the planks butting up against each other, edge to edge, rather than overlapping. Carvel-build technology, because of its stronger framing, produces a sturdier hull, which in turn facilitates greater length and breadth, and allows more complex sail rigs to be adopted. Consequently, Mediterranean galleys were also used as cargo vessels.

From the time of the Phoenicians onwards, navigation of the Mediterranean by galleys is a matter of historical record. There are visual representations of galleys on pottery, artefacts and building decorations from early Egypt onwards, and there is description of the fittings of a luxury gallery in the Old Testament book of Ezekiel, written in around 600 BC.[7] Galleys fought in all the wars of the great Mediterranean sea powers – Greece, Carthage, and Rome – until the fall of the latter's empire in the fifth century.

Medieval maritime warfare witnessed the rise of the Muslim galleys, and those of Venice and Genoa. There were the religious wars of the Crusades and the rise of the Turkish Ottoman empire leading to the 1571 battle of Lepanto, the last significant sea battle between rowing vessels. In this engagement, the Holy Alliance, led by Don John of Austria, was pitted against the Ottoman empire. The Holy Alliance won the day and the Mediterranean, in name, became a Christian-controlled sea.

After Lepanto came the rise of the Barbary corsairs. These were Muslim pirates and privateers out of the coast of North Africa, a loose confederation of North African states, Algiers, Tunis, and Tripoli, and the Moroccan Salee rovers, who terrorised the Mediterranean for three hundred years, taking Christian ships and putting their crews to the oars, just as Christians were taking Muslim ships and subjecting their crews to a similar fate. Thomas Sanders has left an 1854 account of being captured by Muslims and set to the galleys, an account providing an interesting comparison with that of Marteilhe's, although written over a hundred years later. Sanders sailed in the *Jesus* (100 tons) from Portsmouth to Tripoli. In Sanders' memoir, after loading a cargo of 'sweet oils', a dispute arose over customs, the *Jesus* was impounded, and its crew imprisoned. They were first chained 'four and four to an hundredweight of iron,' and then sent to the galleys where:

> Our lodging was bare boards, with only a simple cape for cover. We were also forcibly and most violently shaven, head and beard. . . . Three days later [5 May 1584] myself and six more were sent forth to take a Greek Carmosel and we rowed out of Tripoli 750 miles chained three and three to an oar, and naked above the girdle and cruelly manacled. The Boatswain of the galley walked abaft the mast, and his Mate afore, each with a thong with which, when

their devilish choler arose, they would strike the
Christians for no cause. Our allowance was half-a-
pound of bread a day, without any other sustenance,
except water. We fought the Carmosel for three hours
and took it. We lost but two men, the Greeks had five
slain and fourteen wounded. Those uninjured were
made our slaves and put to the oars, and within
fifteen days we returned to Tripoli; where we were put
to all manner of other slavery.[8]

Back in France in the seventeenth century, Louis XIV
(1638-1715) made use of the galley as a defensive vessel,
as attacks on Christian shipping by Muslims in the
Mediterranean escalated. In 1665 he established a galley
corps, separate from the French navy itself, as a tool of
his royal authority, an extension of both his policies and
aspirations, and a symbol of his power. Officers and
commanders were picked court favourites, members of
the leading rentier families of France, and the Knights
of Malta. The fighting forces on board were French
infantry. At its peak, in 1690, the corps consisted of fifty
active service vessels manned by fifteen thousand crew
drawn from Muslims, criminals, African blacks, representatives of other European nations, and even North
American Iroquois, later joined by the Huguenots.

From its inception until the Revocation of the Edict,
Louis put about seventy million livres into his corps
from a total naval expenditure of 300 million livres.
Why was this money used to construct what was, in

monetary terms, the equivalent of a floating Versailles? The answer can be found not only in the way that Louis conceptualised his kingship – as he expressed it, 'The State, it is I' – but also in the grand design of making the Mediterranean Sea a 'French lake', in the way that, as Louis was well aware, the English were attempting to do the same in many of the seas of the rest of the world. A royal galley corps also represented a way of controlling the court by offering a good salary and easy command possibilities: galleys were usually active only six months a year because they were unfit for winter conditions, and, as Marteilhe tells us, 'A captain has twelve thousand Livres Yearly; and when the Galley is fitted out, he has five hundred Livres a Month for his Table.'[9]

Galleys were also a secure means of incarceration, as well as potentially a means of religious conversion once the Huguenots came on the scene: a means for Louis to increase his standing with both the Pope, and even God. As Bamford writes, they were 'built by the King of France, eldest son of the Church, commanded by the Knights of Malta and (spiritually by the Missionaries) and propelled by Moslem slaves and Protestant heretics – Louis was an active protector-propagator of the Faith.'[10] Galleys provided a conveyor belt from the jails to the grave of free labour, and so relieved the pressure on what rudimentary prison system was then in place. Very few came back from the galleys because there was no one appointed to monitor the length of sentence served: although a prisoner's time might be up, his number was never called and, generally, once aboard, captives were there to die.

After the time of Jean Marteilhe's incarceration in the second decade of the eighteenth century, with the release of the Huguenots, and new treaties with Muslim and other European countries, and the improvement and semi-humanising of prison systems, galley numbers decreased radically. By the 1730s the corps was cut by a third, and many of those vessels remaining were unseaworthy and '[t]he arsenal formerly busy with sounds of carpenters, smiths, and sawyers was now mostly quiet.'[11] The French galley corps was abolished by King Louis XV in 1748, although the galleys were still used as shore-based state prisons. According to Crooke, '[t]he last galleys were built in 1750 and were maintained for two decades. There were still nine galleys on the Navy list in 1773 and one was on campaign in the Mediterranean as late as 1799. Then they were gone forever.'[12]

However, the North African coastal strip was different. Barren, with no industry and little natural resources, the corsairs persisted with the galleys because they had no money or materials for the large square-rigged ships now controlling the seas. And now they were suddenly pirates. In the early nineteenth century, a concerted effort was made by the English, Dutch,

Portuguese and Americans to bring them under control. But '[n]othing but downright conquest could stop the plague, and that final measure was reserved for another nation than the English ... The *coup de grâce* was administered by France.'[13] After this, in 1830, the Mediterranean was brought to an uneasy peace.

Accounts such as that of Marteilhe, or of Thomas Sanders in the nineteenth century, are rare, and we are in possession of Sanders' tale because he was sufficiently educated to leave a witness record. From those who built the pyramids, from indigenous slaves, or from illiterate peasants or criminals, we hear nothing. To hear a voice from where voices are not usually heard there must be an educated, literate involvement, which brings us back to Marteilhe. Once the Huguenots began to be condemned to the galleys we had eyes that could see, hands that could record, money that could publish. We had, in fact, Marteilhe's *Memoirs*.

Jean Marteilhe was born at Bergerac in 1684, into an affluent and educated family. In the autobiography he passes over his childhood, beginning his story in his seventeenth year, in 1700, when the French court gives the Duke de La Force permission to 'convert' all the Huguenots of Bergerac to Catholicism. La Force quarters twenty-two dragoons in the Marteilhe home, and these 'after having consumed and destroyed everything', send Marteilhe's father to prison, put his siblings

in a convent, and torture his mother to sign a renunciation of her faith. Marteilhe sneaks away that night
from Bergerac, with a friend: they intend to try to cross
France and reach Holland and freedom, but after many
hair's breadth escapes they are betrayed and arrested.
Holland was their goal because of the welcome accorded
to the Huguenot refugees: 'if Catholic France showed
herself without bowels of compassion for her proscribed
children, in Holland they found a new country, which
ended by solemnly adopting them, and abolishing all
distinction between them and its own citizens.'[14] They
confess to being Huguenots, but not to trying to escape
from France. Marteilhe says, 'Alas may God pardon us
that we were weak and foolish . . . but such is human
nature, which never performs a good work perfectly.'

Confined to prison, and slowly starving, two further
Huguenot prisoners arrive, 'fellow-townsmen' of
Marteilhe who have money, but the new arrivals confess
that to gain their freedom they have renounced their
religion. This means that on their release, they will be
free to return to Bergerac with news of Marteilhe's
capture and whereabouts. From that time, the Marteilhe
family money can be made available to 'grease the paw'
of various gaolers and galley officials, although there
can be no absolute freedom without their signing a
'renunciation.' Marteilhe, however, emphasises to the
reader his willingness and determination to suffer for his
adherence to his faith and, by implication, retain his

integrity. Through all his various vicissitudes Marteilhe tells us that he is repeatedly offered freedom in return for his renunciation of Protestantism and conversion to Catholicism, and his firm refusals sees him eventually 'fettered in irons', and marched off to join the fleet of six galleys at Dunkirk, stationed there to counter Dutch and British movements at sea during the offensive against the French in the Low Countries. However, he pictures these religious tensions as being characterised by hypocrisy: many of those who help him during his imprisonment are described as having converted to Catholicism for the sake of expediency, yet in their heart remaining sympathetic to the Protestant cause.

To complement Marteilhe's description of life on the galleys, there is also one extant written by John Bion (Jean-François Bion), a sometime Catholic priest to the galleys at Marseilles, who eventually fled to England, becoming a Protestant convert. He affirms Marteilhe's account of the harsh conditions endured by the crews of the galleys, telling us of the exposed conditions on deck. Bion writes:

> A Galley is a long, flat one-decked vessel, though it hath two masts. They generally make use of the oars, because they are not able to endure a rough sea; and therefore their sails are for the most part useless. There are five slaves to every oar; one of them a Turk; who being generally stronger than the Christians, is set at the upper end, to work it with more strength.

Generally, in all, there are 300 slaves; and 250 men,
either officers, soldiers, seamen, or servants. There is,
in the stern of the galley, a chamber shaped on the
outside like a cradle, belonging to the captain: and
solely his, at night or in foul weather; but in the
daytime common to all officers and the chaplain. The
rest of the crew are exposed above decks, to the
scorching heat of the sun by day, and the damps and
inclemencies of the night. There is a kind of tent
suspended by a cable from head to stern, that affords
some little shelter: but only in fair weather when they
can best be without it. The least wind or storm it is
taken down; the galley not being able to carry it for
fear of oversetting.'[15]

Jean Barras de La Penne (1650-1730) was first rear
admiral of the galleys of Louis XIV, and from 1729
commander of the port of Marseilles. Writing in 1713, he
also gives us an account of other aspects of life on an
eighteenth-century galley, and vividly depicts the
crowded conditions on board. He tells us that '[t]hose
who see a galley for the first time are astonished at so
many persons; there being an infinite number of villages
in Europe without as many inhabitants.' He also speaks
of the lack of space this causes, saying that '[i]t is true
there is little room to sleep for they put seven men on
one bench – a space about ten feet long by four feet
broad . . . At the bow one sees some thirty sailors who
have for their lodgings a platform about ten foot by

eight . . . The captain and officers are scarcely better lodged, and one is tempted to compare their grandeur with Diogenes in his tub.'[16]

De La Penne depicts life on the galley as a form of hell on earth for the criminal classes, while his description of the lack of seaworthiness of these vessels during a storm has an apocalyptic tone:

> . . . everything combines to make life hell. The creaking of the blocks, the cries of the sailors, the horrible maledictions of the slaves, the groaning of the timbers, the clank of the chains, the rain, hail, lightning and the waves that dash all over the vessel – and while devotion is not, as a rule, strongly marked on a galley – you will hear these folk praying to God who would be much better not to forget God once danger is past.'[17]

Yet there is no escaping the horrors, whatever the weather. Calm also poses its problems, too, 'the evil smells being so strong that one cannot get away from them in spite of the tobacco with which one is obliged to plug up one's nostrils from morning to night.'[18]

Not only are the physical conditions nigh on unbearable, the prisoners are also punished with violence for their perceived misdemeanours on board. On Marteilhe's first day aboard his galley at Dunkirk, he witnesses 'the terrible punishment of the bastinado', and Bion also leaves a graphic account of this form of punishment:

Every man's chains were taken off and they were put into the hands of four Turks, who stripped them naked, and stretched them on the *Coursier*, the great gun, so they could not so much as stir. During this time, there is a horrid silence throughout the whole galley . . . even the most profligate wretches turning away their eyes. The victim thus prepared, the Turk pitched on to be executioner, with a tough cudgel or knotty rope's end, unmercifully beats the poor wretch; and that more willingly, because he thinks it acceptable to MAHOMAT. But the most barbarous of all is that after the skin is flayed off their bones; the only balsam applied is a mixture of vinegar and salt. After which they are thrown in the hospital lately described.[19]

Marteilhe describes his own narrow escape from being bastinadoed; although Marteilhe suffers cruelly during his imprisonment, by implication he attributes his survival both to the money he receives from the network of Protestant sympathisers, and also to his own personal integrity, appreciated even by his captors. On the galley, *La Palme*, whose comite (overseer or whip-master) is notorious for his cruelty, Marteilhe is heavily chained, but the comite orders his chain to be struck off – Marteilhe's money has travelled before him, and he is assigned to the comite's own bench, an appointment which carries such attractions such as being eligible for the scraps from the comite's table, and a position so sought-after that gaining it was known as being appointed to 'the reserved seats'. Slaves at the comite's bench were never lashed. Even so, Marteilhe emphasises to the reader his refusal to 'dance attendance' on the comite, who calls him to one side and tells him he must make Marteilhe an example by sending him to another bench, but that Marteilhe will never receive a blow from him or his two assistants. Marteilhe is duly grateful, especially as the comite, in action, would have 'whipped his own father'.

Marteilhe also takes pains to make clear to the reader that without slaves and physical abuse the galleys could not have been moved:

A Crew of free Men could not hold out. In the Year 1703 there were built at Dunkirk four half-Galleys to be rowed to Antwerp. Proportioned exactly to larger Gallies but that their oars were twenty five Feet long, and three Men to every Oar. They put in free-Men, perfectly acquainted with rowing; for it was not thought advisable to trust to Slaves, who might be tempted to escape on to the Continent. But when they came to row, they could scarcely leave Port, and the Commander was obliged to write to the Ministry of the Impossibility of navigating without a Crew of Slaves. Upon which a Slave was placed as the first Rower – and then they were able to bring the Vessels from Dunkirk – but only to Ostend, as the Comite could not exercise the same Cruelties on free Men as he did upon Slaves. An incident that proves a Galley cannot be moved without Slaves, and without a Comite. For when a Comite is wanted, the Captain desires no more in a Candidate but Barbarity and Want of Pity. And any who has these Talents, especially in a supreme Degree, is engaged without further Examination.[20]

Funds to bribe the officials were sent by rich Huguenots from Amsterdam to trusted agents and bankers at the galley ports of Marseille and Dunkirk. In Dunkirk, the agent would pass on the monies to Marteilhe to distribute among the Huguenot slaves. As bringing such money on board the galley became extremely dangerous, with Jesuit spies always on watch, Marteilhe eventually makes use of a Turk, Isouf, who rows on his bench to collect the money, the Turkish slaves being allowed ashore. Isouf serves Marteilhe for several years 'without ever accepting the smallest reward', until killed in an engagement. In Marteilhe's eyes, Isouf the Turk, the representative of another race and religion, is characterised by an unselfish integrity and willingness to serve others without recompense, and stands in stark contrast to the way in which he depicts the Catholic clergy of Marteilhe's own nation as hypocritical and self-seeking.

Marteilhe tells us how in 1702 six Dunkirk galleys attack and take a Dutch ship and bring her into Ostend. Bion also writes of the method of attack for a galley on such a ship, and he makes quite clear to us the advantages and drawbacks of the galley in battle.

> I might also observe how in every galley there are five guns upon the foredeck. Viz., four six or eight pounders; and a fifth, this *Coursier*, which carrieth a 36lb ball. And when an enemies ship is becalmed, a galley, which with her oars can do as she pleaseth, may attack that ship fore and aft, to avoide her broadsides, and ply her with the *Coursier*, so that sometimes, if she happeneth to give a shot that comes betwixt wind and water; she forceth a surrender. Which happens seldom enough for any ship needs but little wind to make nothing of overthrowing five or six galleys.[21]

Marteilhe's account of the Dunkirk galleys' encounter with Dutch warships assuming the guise of heavily-laden merchant ships, which ended in over two hundred galley crews dead and many more wounded, demonstrates the disadvantages even more graphically.

In 1708, the squadron cruises the English coast, joined by an Englishman, Captain Smith, a man whom Marteilhe is determined that the reader will see as a thoroughly dishonest character, 'a concealed Papist given charge of the squadron by the French king', who plans to pillage Harwich. They go to sea, and off Harwich see thirty-five merchantmen heading for the Thames, convoyed by a frigate of thirty-six guns, the *Nightingale*. Langeron, the leader of the squadron, decides to take the merchant fleet, overruling Smith's plans for Harwich. This episode, which was one of the last galley actions in northern Europe, ends in disaster, and Marteilhe vividly recaptures the tension of the battle for the reader, and the powerlessness of the slaves chained to the benches to intervene actively in their fate.

Marteilhe tells us that his injuries are so serious that he is almost thrown overboard as dead, but is discovered and put into the bottom of the hold where he lies among the dead, dying, and the 'dreadful stench and gangrene' until he reaches Dunkirk where they are 'hauled up out of the hold with ropes and pulleys, like cattle, and taken to the naval hospital'. Here, once Marteilhe's financial position becomes known, the head surgeon consents to treat Marteilhe personally. Of the rest, three-quarters die, even though not as dangerously wounded as Marteilhe who, at the end of three months, is 'as sleek and fat as a monk'. Once again he singles himself out, hero of his own story, chosen survivor of persecution and suffering. As Marteilhe shows us so graphically, medical facilities on the galleys were less than rudimentary. Bion confirms this in his horrifying description of the suffering of the sick on his galley:

> There is in the hold, a close dark room, the only passage being a scuttle two feet square, through

which air is also admitted. At each end of this room is a sort of scaffold called a *Taular*; on which the sick are laid, promiscuously, without beds or anything under them. In this place all kind of vermin gnaw these poor creatures without disturbance. When twice daily called among them, to confess, advise, or administer to the dying I was instantly covered all over. The only way was to wear a night gown, and to strip it off on exiting. . . . In there, confessing those ready to expire, the whole space between the ceiling and *Taular* being but three feet; I was obliged to lie down by their sides and often as I was confessing one, another would expire next to me. . . . The stench is intolerable, and there is no slave, howeverso weak, but would rather expire at his oar, in chains, than end in this loathsome place.[22]

To be sick or wounded is to endure yet another form of degradation and suffering, even worse than slaving at the oars.

In 1709 we see Marteilhe returned to duty but, because of his wounds, unable to row. He is first made a storekeeper, then becomes the commander's secretary and as a rich trustee he is well-treated for the next three years. In 1711 France and Great Britain came to terms, prior to the Treaty of Utrecht, and Britain acquired Dunkirk. The long War of Spanish Succession was over. Marteilhe tells us that an English fleet arrives in Dunkirk in September 1712, with about five thousand men, all of whom immediately 'ran in crowds to gaze upon the galleys', and who are violently angry at the treatment of the Protestants. One of the English commanders, 'Lord Hill',[23] instructs Marteilhe to draw up a petition to be presented to Queen Anne, but according to Marteilhe, Hill then betrays the Huguenot galley slaves, suggesting to Langeron that the slaves should be removed to Marseilles to prevent the trouble that might ensue from a rescue attempt by the English ordinary seamen. The religious conflict is thus elided into one of class.

Accordingly, at the beginning of October 1712, the Huguenots among the galley slaves are 'smuggled off' from Dunkirk to be sent to the galleys of Marseilles, via Calais and Havre. The treatment on land is pictured as even worse than the treatment on sea: in the grim prison where they pause along the way, the slaves are chained by the neck to huge beams of oak lying on the floor, so they can neither 'sit nor lie', and any who cry out are beaten with 'huge ox bones.' Once again, the power of money to alleviate their suffering is emphasised, and some relief is eventually purchased; eventually in December the chain leaves for Marseilles, a rich Parisian Huguenot paying 'one hundred crowns to buy us off from blows.'

Yet the power of money only travels so far: en route, one frosty night in a freezing wind, the slaves are ordered to strip in the courtyard of an inn. After having all of their belongings stolen from their clothes, they are kept standing naked through the night. Ordered to reform, all are 'so stiffened by cold' they cannot walk; they are cudgelled and whipped, some dying in the process. They arrive at Marseilles in January 1713, Marteilhe commenting he had suffered more between Dunkirk and Marseilles, than 'during the twelve previous years.' At Marseilles they are placed in the galley *Grande Réale* where they come under great pressure from the Jesuits to convert, the Jesuits apparently having heard that Queen Anne of England is, in turn, now interesting herself in the cause of the Huguenots and pressuring the King of France for their release.

Eventually the Peace of Utrecht is signed and a petition organised by the Marquis de Rochegude is delivered to Queen Anne, whom he waylays in St James's Park. Diplomacy creaks into action, and at the end of May 1713 an order comes to the Governor of Marseilles to release one hundred and thirty-six Huguenots. However, Marteilhe's narrative keeps the reader in suspense right until the last pages, and his escape from the clutches of his captors seems by no means assured until the very end of his account. The Jesuits fight the order for release at court, but with no success, and eventually, with the assistance of a sea-captain determined to help them to overcome the final obstacles put in their way, the chosen Huguenots set sail, disembarking at Villafranca and journeying overland to Geneva, where the description is of a heroes' welcome. From Geneva, they travel to Frankfurt, Cologne, and then Amsterdam, 'the termination of our long journey' and finally we see these prisoners of conscience safe from persecution at last.

In this introduction we have heard the voices of galley slaves, a galley priest, and La Penne, who was the equivalent of a shore superintendent, but what has not been heard is the voice of any galley commander, perhaps because of an understandable reluctance on the part of commanders to admit, in writing, to having supervised such an institution. However, we do have one account of everyday life in the great cabin, left by the young Carlo Gozzi, who travelled for a short time as a favourite in a Venetian galley of the period, and which is worth quoting at length because of its unique and individual insight into life upon the galleys from the other side of the bench. Gozzi's brother procured him a place on the *Generalizia*, the flagship of Girolamo Quirini, general-designate of armaments for the Adriatic. Like many young men since, Gozzi, 'guitar and books' in hand, joins his first ship:

> I embarked on the *Generalizia* to be received by the military officers with both courtesy and curiosity. In a court where all seek preferment, any newcomer is heavily scrutinised should a promotion become available. Such thoughts being ever-present wood-worms in the hearts of courtiers. I had to answer a

quantity of questions . . . but as some knew my brother, I was eventually welcomed with noisy demonstrations of comradeship. I expressed thanks in modest phrases, and retired to study their characters. Some were men of birth and liberal culture. Some were nobles, ruined by the worst of educations. Others were commoners, owing their positions to powerful protection. As to their habits – gambling, intemperance, and unbridled sensuality. Vices which clung to them like ineradicable cancers. Sound principles from early years; a regard for my health; and slenderness of purse; helped me avoid these seductions. At the same time, I saw no reason to proclaim a crusade. Holding a middle course, I won their affections; and they invited me to their orgies; where I laughed at their drunken antics while quietly observing their animal brutality.

Waiting for Quirini to arrive, I also spent time reflecting on another aspect of humanity – the galley slaves. Three hundred or so scoundrels, loaded with chains, and condemned to drag out their lives in a sea of miseries and torments, each sufficient by itself to kill a man. For at this time a malignant fever was raging among them, carrying away its victim daily from their bread and water; and the irons and whips of their slavemasters. In this, their last passage, they were attended by a gaunt Franciscan friar, with a thundering voice and jovial mien. And it was with his exhortations ringing in their ears that these poor wretches took their flight – I hope to paradise.

I was aroused from these dismal reveries by the arrival of Quirini. Appearing in a crimson cape, cap and shoes, businesslike and fierce, he came on board amidst the din of instruments and roar of cannons. I had visited this person at least ten times in his own palace, and had always been warmly welcomed. Now all were bowing 'til their noses touched their toes as, looking at none, he sentenced a young captain of the guards to arrest in chains, because of an omission of some trifling military salute. Perhaps he felt bound to assume a totally different aspect to that natural to him – to inspire fear and submission in his subordinates – who, being presumptuous young fellows, might otherwise have been inclined to take liberties on the strength of his former courtesy.

Eventually he retired to his cabin in the bowels of this floating hell, and sent lieutenant-colonel Micheli to make a list of all officers; and the names of their protectors. Nobody expected this – having all been previously presented to Quirini – but I reflected this could be a further way of damping expectations that might be breeding in scheming brains. Everybody began to grumble as Micheli – excellent, but very fat – bustled about, sweating and scribbling as though it were a matter of life or death – as, for him, it may well have been. When my turn came, I stated frankly I was Carlo Gozzi; recommended by the Almoro Cesare Tiepolo. (I deemed it prudent to withhold his title of Senator; and him being my uncle.)

Shortly after, the *Generalizia* got under way. Soon

it grew dark and necessity making me seek some corner, I was directed to the bowsprit. On approaching it, I was greeted by an Illyrian sentinel with scowling visage and bushy whiskers who levelled his musket; while simultaneously howling in a tremendous voice: 'Who goes there?' On understanding my business, he let me pass. My next step was onto a soft and yielding mass which gave out a kind of gurgling sound, like the breath of an asthmatic patient. After dealing with my needs, I retraced my path, asking the sentinel what it was that had gurgled to the pressure of my feet. He answered with complete indifference it was the corpse of a galley slave who had died of fever, and had been flung there.

After twelve days and nights of extreme discomfort, we entered the harbour of Zara. Here Quirini would receive the baton of command – overseen by another old fat man, Girolamo Visinoni – appointed master of ceremonies on account of his intimate acquaintance with their details. Observances which were eventually performed to the sound of military music, and crackling of musket shots; and were well-deserved to be witnessed by any interested in such spectacles. I myself had no duty that day but to wear my best clothes, which I did without much trouble.[24]

Unlike Gozzi, Marteilhe never sat in the great cabin of a galley as a guest, but nor did he end up as a 'soft and yielding' corpse, to be trodden underfoot, and he escaped death to leave us his account as a survivor and a witness.

His situation and account has parallels with that of the writer, Primo Levi (1919-87), who was a Jewish prisoner in the Auschwitz concentration camp during the second world war, and, like Marteilhe, wrote a memoir of his experiences. Just as Marteilhe's socioeconomic background helped to ensure his eventual survival, and provided him with the ability to leave a written record as witness of his experience, so too did Levi's education gain him indoor work in an industrial complex rather than remaining in the camp, keeping him from freezing winter temperatures and almost certain death. This education also enabled his recording of his time as prisoner: both men are not only survivors of the most terrible imprisonment, but also witnesses, voices in history recording their suffering as representatives of a class of people, so that these sufferings might not be forgotten in the mists of time. As Levi writes, 'We who survived the camps are not true witnesses. We are those who, through prevarication, skill or luck, never touched bottom. Those who did, and saw the face of the Gorgon, did not return; or returned wordless.'[25]

Marteilhe's words stand witness not only for his own personal trials in the French galleys, but also enable us to gain some insight into the trials of all of those imprisoned on the galleys in the eighteenth century, whether imprisoned as common criminals or prisoners of conscience, those silent and willing Turkish slaves and the other nameless prisoners on these floating gaols.

Marteilhe's account also sheds light on the plight of the French Huguenots and the way that they perceived their persecutions, as well as the powerlessness of the common man caught up in a world of military and political manoeuvring, directed by remote and aristocratic figures from afar. His words tell us not only of him personally, but also tell a tale of the voiceless and the oppressed, and are thus still worth preserving and reading three centuries after they were written.

Galley Slave

Foreword: A description of a galley, its crew, and method of fighting

BEFORE I DETAIL the many miseries endured on the galleys, some of the names of the parts of the galley and its officers that occur in the course of this narrative should perhaps be detailed to the reader.

A galley is ordinarily a hundred and fifty feet long, and fifty feet broad. It consists of but one deck, which deck covers the hold. This hold is, in the middle, seven feet deep, but at the sides of the galley only six feet. By this we may see that the deck rises about a foot in the middle, and slopes towards the edges, to let the water run off more easily: for when a galley is loaded, it seems to swim under water, at least the sea constantly washes the deck. The sea would then necessarily enter the hold by the apertures where the masts are placed, were it not prevented by what is called the coursier. This is a long case of boards fixed on the middle, or highest part of the deck, and running from one end of the galley to the other. There is also a hatchway into the hold, as high as the coursier.

From this superficial description, perhaps it may be imagined that the slaves and the crew always have their feet in water. But this is not so; to each rower's bench there is a board raked a foot from the deck, which serves as a footstool to the rowers, and under which the water passes.

For the soldiers and mariners there is, running down each side of the ship, along the gunnels, what is called the bande, which is a bench of about the same height with the coursier, and two feet broad. They never lie here, but each leans on his own particular bundle of clothes, in a very uncomfortable posture. Nor are the officers better accommodated, for the six chambers in the hold are designed only to hold the provisions, and naval stores of the galley.

The hold
The hold is divided into six apartments.

One: The gavon – a little cabin near the poop which is big enough only to hold the captain's bed.

Two: The escantiolat – where the captain's provisions are kept and dressed.

Three: The compagne – this contains the beer, wine, oil, vinegar and fresh water of the whole crew, together with their bacon, salted meat, fish and cheese: they never use butter.

Four: The paillot – here are kept the dried provisions, as biscuit, peas, rice, etc.

Five: The tavern – this apartment is in the middle of the galley. It contains the wine which is retailed by the comite, and of which he enjoys the profits. This opens into the powder room, of which the gunner alone keeps the key. In this chamber also the sails and tents are kept.

Six: The steerage – where the cordage and the surgeon's chest are kept. It also serves during a voyage as a hospital for the sick and wounded, who, however, have no other bed to lie on than ropes. In winter, when the galley is laid-up, the sick are sent to a hospital in the city.

A galley has fifty benches for rowers: twenty-five each side. Each bench is ten feet long; one end fixed in the coursier, the other in the bande. The benches are half a foot thick, and placed at four feet distant from each other. They are covered with sackcloth, fluffed with flocks, and over this is thrown a cowhide, which, reaching down to the banquet, or footstool, gives them the resemblance of large trunks. To these benches the slaves are chained, six to a bench. Along the bande runs a large rim of timber, about a foot thick, which forms the gunnel of the galley: to this, the oars are fixed. These oars are fifty feet long, and are poised in equilibrium upon the aforementioned timber, so that the thirteen feet of oar which comes into the galley, is equal in weight to the thirty-seven which go into the water. As it would be impossible to hold the oars in the hand, because of their thickness, they have handles, by which they are managed by the slaves.

Galley Slave

The method of sailing a galley

The comite, who is master of the slaves, and a tyrant much dreaded, stands always at the stern, near the captain, to receive his orders. There are also two sous-comites, or under-comites: one in the middle, the other near the prow. Each of these carries a whip of cords which they exercise without mercy on the naked bodies of the slaves. The two sous-comites are always immediately attentive to the orders of the comite. When the captain gives the word for rowing, the comite gives the signal with a silver whistle, which hangs from his neck: this is repeated by the sous-comite, at which the slaves, who have their oars in readiness, strike all at once, and beat time exactly, that the fifty oars seem to give but one blow.

Thus they continue, without requiring further orders, till by another signal of the whistle, they desist in a moment. There is an absolute necessity for thus rowing all together, for should one of the oars be lifted up, or fall too soon, those in front, in leaning back, will necessarily strike the oar behind them with the hinder part of their heads; while the struck slaves will do the same to those behind them.

But it were well if a few bruises on the head was the only punishment: the comites exercise their whips on such an occasion like furies, while the muscles of the slaves, all in convulsions under the lash, pour streams of blood down onto the seats. This, however dreadful it may seem to the reader, is soon learned by the slaves, by regular usage, to be born without murmuring.

'To labour like a galley-slave' is a proverb, and it may be reckoned the greatest fatigue that can be inflicted on beings already wretched. Imagine six men chained to their seats, naked as when born, sitting with one foot on a block of timber, fixed to the footstool or stretcher, the other lifted up against the bench before them, holding in their hands an oar of an enormous size. Imagine them lengthening their bodies, their arms stretched out to push the oar over the backs of those before them, who are also themselves in a similar attitude. Having thus advanced their oar, they raise that end which they hold in their hands, to plunge the opposite in the sea; which done, they throw themselves back upon their benches below, which are somewhat hollowed to receive them. None, in short, but those who have seen them labour, can conceive how much they endure.

None such begin to believe that human strength could sustain the fatigue which they undergo for hours successively. But what cannot necessity and cruelty make men do? Certain it is, that a galley cannot be navigated, but by a crew of slaves, over whom a comite may exercise the most unbounded authority. No free man could continue at the oar an hour unwearied: yet a slave must sometimes lengthen out his toil for ten, twelve, nay, for twenty hours, without the smallest intermission. On these occasions the comite, or some of the other mariners, put into the mouths of those wretches a bit of bread steeped in wine, to prevent fainting through excess of fatigue or hunger, while their hands are employed upon the oar. At such times are heard nothing but horrid blasphemies, loud bursts of despair or ejaculations to heaven; all accompanied by terrible threats, and the cracking of whips on flesh, to fill up this dreadful harmony.

Now the captain roars to the comite to redouble his blows; and when any one drops from his oar in a faint, which not unfrequently happens, he is whipped while any remains of life appear, and then thrown into the sea without further ceremony. But how much happier is he than those unpitied wretches he leaves behind! Perhaps Heaven was pleased to give him all his punishment here in the galleys, with a view to rewarding him with a happy immortality.

The bursts of anguish which I have felt, at seeing my brother Protestants thus inhumanly butchered, can never leave my mind. Yet I will cease lamenting; they want not my tears, nor any human compassion, to add to their present felicity in Paradise.

1. Flight and capture 1700-1701

ALMOST ALL OF MY fellow Huguenots would bear witness to the bloody and cruel persecutions inflicted upon them in every part of France since the year 1684. Many have written about it in a general way, but no one (at least to my knowledge) has particularised the different kinds of hardship and torture to be experienced in the galleys. I shall therefore impart what befell myself in those vessels, from the year 1700 to the year 1713, at which time I was happily delivered by God's mercy, and by the intercession of Anne of England.

I was born in 1684, at Bergerac, a small town in the province of Perigord. My parents were in trade, but brought up their children as Huguenots in the true reformed religion – Protestantism. I will not weary my reader by relating the events of my childhood; but pass to my flight from my home, and what occasioned it.

During the Nine Years' War which terminated in the Peace of Ryswick (1697), the Jesuits had not been able to indulge in the pleasure of harassing the Huguenots with the King's troops, because the latter were needed to guard the kingdom. But no sooner was peace concluded, than these pitiless soldiers made their rage felt throughout France.

In 1699, the Duke de La Force[26] requested permission from the court to go to his estates in Perigord, in order, as he expressed it, 'to convert' the Huguenots. This permission was granted and La Force immediately set out from Paris, accompanied by four Jesuits, guards and servants. Arrived at his castle, about three miles from Bergerac, La Force began to exercise unheard-of cruelties against Huguenots on his estates. Peasants of every age, and both sexes, were made to suffer, without trial, the most terrible tortures to compel them to renounce their religion, and then, by means as equally diabolical, to take the most fearful oaths to remain attached to the Roman Church. To testify the joy and satisfaction which he felt at his successes, and to terminate his enterprise in a manner he felt worthy of his motives, La Force made a bonfire of a magnificent library of Protestant books which his ancestors (all Protestants themselves) had carefully collected.

At this, I must amuse my reader with a scene which took place at the castle, where La Force was reposing after his fatigues, while receiving the praises of the priests and monks of the neighbourhood. There was an advocate of Bergerac, named Grenier. This man was a wit, but also a little mad. He expressed a wish to join the other flatterers, and was admitted to audience. La Force was sitting in his chair of state, his four Jesuits[27] by his side.

Grenier began in these words: 'Monseigneur, your grandfather was a great warrior, your father a great saint, while you, Monseigneur, are a great huntsman.' The Duke, who had no great passion for the chase, here interrupted to inquire how Grenier judged that he, the Duke, was a great huntsman.

'I judge of it,' replied Grenier, pointing to the Jesuits, 'by your four bloodhounds.' Immediately they heard this, the fathers, like good Christians, demanded that Grenier be severely punished. But as it was represented that Grenier was not right in his mind, La Force was content with simply driving the advocate from his presence.

After this, the Duke returned to Paris to render an account of his successes to the court, successes that obtained for him permission to return to Perigord in October 1700, to convert, by any means, the Huguenots in *all* the royal towns of that province. He eventually came to Bergerac, accompanied by the same four Jesuits, and a regiment of dragoons. The cruelties of these latter made a great many more converts than the exhortations of the Jesuits, as there were no measures these booted and spurred missionaries did not exercise to oblige the citizens to go to Mass.

Twenty-two of these dragoons were quartered with my father, and after having consumed and destroyed everything in the house, my father was cast into prison, while two of my brothers, and my sister, still children, were placed in a convent. I had the good fortune to escape from the house before they entered it, but this left my poor mother in the midst of those twenty-two wretches, who caused her to undergo horrible tortures before dragging her before La Force who, with infamous treatment, presented the form of renunciation for her signature. Though weeping abundantly, she signed. But after writing her name at the bottom, she added: '(La) Force made me do it', alluding to the Duke. They tried to make her efface these words, but as she persisted in refusing, one of the Jesuits did so for her.

Knowing myself in great danger, and just sixteen years of age, I left the town after dark, accompanied by a friend, Daniel Le Gras, a hairdresser. After walking all night through the woods, we found ourselves the next morning at Mussidan, a small town twelve miles from Bergerac. There we resolved, whatever the perils, to try to reach the safety of Holland. We implored divine protection for our journey, and vowed we would remain firm and constant in confessing the Protestant religion, even at the risk of the galleys, or death. After making a firm resolution not to imitate Lot's wife[28] by looking back, we proceeded cheerfully along the high road to Paris, although not too well supplied with money – our whole capital being about ten pistoles.[29]

After lodging every day at the humblest inns, we eventually reached Paris on 10 November 1699. Here we expected to meet some of our acquaintances, and learn the easiest and least dangerous route to the frontier. A good friend drew us a map as far as Mézières, a garrison town on the River Meuse, at that time the frontier of the Spanish Netherlands, beyond which was the formidable forest of Ardennes, and beyond which lay Charleroi, and freedom. He informed us that the great danger would be entering Mézières – because they were extremely particular at the gate in stopping strangers, and those found without passports were taken at once before the governor, and thence to prison. But on leaving Mézières, he added, no one was ever stopped. And once through Mézières, the forest of Ardennes would favour our journey to Charleroi, twenty-six or so miles away, when we should then be out of the French territories. Our friend added that at Charleroi there was also a Dutch garrison whose commander would protect us from all danger.

We started from Paris for Mézières. Nothing occurred en route, for within the French dominions no one was ever stopped, the government concentrating only on the borders. We arrived then, one afternoon, about four o'clock, at the summit of a little hill, about three-quarters of a mile from Mézières. From here we could see the whole of the town and the gate by which we should have to enter, this latter being approached by a long bridge over the River Meuse. As it was very fine weather, a number of the inhabitants were walking about on the bridge. We thought that by mixing with these citizens, we should be able to enter the town without attracting attention. We emptied our knapsacks of our few shirts and put them all on, putting our knapsacks into our pockets. We then cleaned our shoes, and combed our hair, so as not to look like travellers. We had no swords, for that was then forbidden in France. We descended the hill and walked up and down the bridge with the citizens, until the drum beat for the closing of the gates, at which all the inhabitants hastened to return into the town, and we with them. We were filled with joy when the sentinel ignored us, but the gate leading out of the town, being shut at the same time, meant we must now lodge for the night.

Entering the first inn that presented itself, we were met by the landlord's wife. We ordered supper; and whilst at table, at about nine o'clock, the landlord arrived back. From our chamber, we heard his wife tell him she had received two young strangers. Her husband immediately asked if we had a ticket of permission from the governor. His wife replied that she had not inquired.

'Slut!' said he. 'Do you wish to ruin us utterly? You know the prohibitions against lodging strangers. They must come with me at once to the governor.' He then entered our chamber, and asked very civilly if we had spoken to the governor. We told him that we had not thought this necessary when lodging for only one night.

'It would cost me a thousand crowns,' said he, 'if the governor knew that I had lodged you without his permission. But you do have the passport necessary to

enter frontier towns?' We replied that we were well
furnished with papers.

'Hopefully that will be enough. Still, you must come
with me to the governor to show your passports.' We
replied that we were very fatigued; but that next morning we would willingly accompany him. He appeared
satisfied and left.

We finished our supper, and though our bed was a
good one, it did not induce sleep, so troubled were we
by the perils that threatened next day. We talked quietly
through the night of the answers we should make to the
governor, but saw nothing in front of us, but going
straight from the governor's house to prison. We finally
decided our only chance was to escape at dawn. As light
began to break, we got up and dressed quickly, and
crept down to the kitchen, to find this was where the
landlord and his wife slept. He immediately awoke, and
seeing us about so early, inquired the reason.

We said that having to go to the governor, we wished
to breakfast as soon as possible, so on leaving the
governor's we could proceed onwards at once. The
landlord approved our scheme, and ordered his servant
to fry some sausages, while he, the landlord, made his
toilet. This kitchen was on the ground floor, close to the
street door which the servant now opened. Making a
pretext that we wished to go out for a few moments, and
without saying farewell, or paying our reckoning, we
found a little boy, of whom we asked the way to the

Charleville gate, by which we could leave the town. We were very near it, and as the gate was open we went out without any obstacle.

On reaching Charleville, a small town with neither gate nor garrison, and within gunshot of Mézières, we breakfasted quickly, and then left it to enter the safety of the forest of Ardennes. It had frozen during the night, and the trees appeared terrible, covered with hoar frost and icicles. As we penetrated this vast forest we were confronted with a great number of roads. Not knowing which led to Charleroi, we asked the way of a peasant we met. His answer was that for strangers to go to Charleroi by way of the Ardennes forest was very dangerous, as the further we advanced the more roads we should meet. And as there was neither village nor house in this great wood, we might wander about for twelve or fifteen days. And that if the frost continued we might perish there of cold and hunger, plus the forest was full of ravenous animals. We offered the peasant a gold louis if he would serve as a guide to Charleroi.

'Not if you were to offer me a hundred,' he said. 'I think that you are Huguenots trying to escape from France, and helping you would only put a rope round my own neck.' Although he would not guide us, he gave us good advice to leave the forest, and detailed various villages through which we should have to pass to Charleroi. 'A route,' he ended, 'longer than that by the

Ardennes, but without any danger.'

We thanked this good man and in the evening we arrived at the first village of which he spoke. We slept there, and next morning continued on the next road he suggested. This led us straight to a narrow gorge, called the Guet du Sud, between two mountains, where there was a guardhouse of French soldiers, with a sentinel in front of it, stopping all strangers and asking for passports. Like poor straying sheep, we had walked into the jaws of the wolf. We had been seen, and so had to go forward, but then, by the most favourable chance, rain began to fall so heavily that the sentinel went into the guardhouse for shelter, and we passed by quite innocently. And pursuing our way, arrived at the town of Couve.

At that moment we were safe, had we only known it, as this little town was not on French territory. It belonged to the Prince of Liège,[30] and contained a castle garrisoned by Dutch troops, the governor of which granted an escort to all refugees to conduct them to Charleroi. But it was God's will that we should remain in ignorance, so that our faith should be put to the trial during thirteen years of dungeons and galleys, as will be seen in the course of these memoirs.

We arrived, then, at Couve, wet to the skin. We entered an inn to dry ourselves, and to get something to eat. Having sat down to table, they brought us a pot of beer with two handles, without giving us any glasses.

On asking for some, the host said that he perceived we were Frenchmen, for the custom of that country was to drink out of the pot. But this request for glasses, which seemed at the time a mere trifle, was the cause of our ruin, for in the same room with us were two men: one an ordinary citizen, the other a gamekeeper of the Prince of Liège. The latter, noticing the observation of the landlord, began to examine us very carefully, and at last declared he was ready to lay a wager that we did not carry rosaries in our pockets. That is, we were not Catholics.

My companion, at that moment taking a pinch of snuff, gestured to his snuff box, saying that that was his rosary. This reply told the gamekeeper what he wanted to know: that we were Protestants, attempting to escape from France. And as the belongings of those arrested belonged to the informer, and he thought we had money, he conceived the design of following us when we left Couve, in the hope we would pass through Mariembourg, about three miles away, but back in French territory.

On leaving Couve, we should have taken the road to the left, by which we should have avoided touching French territory. But coming towards us along that road we perceived an officer on horseback. And as the least thing increases fear, lest this officer should stop us, we turned and took the fatal road to Mariembourg – a small town with only one gate, so there is no direct passage through it. Still unaware of the treacherous gamekeeper we arrived when it was almost dark, and entered through the gate. There was an inn opposite. We went in, they gave us a room, and we had a good fire made to dry ourselves. After about half an hour a man came in who saluted us very civilly, then asked whence we came, and whither we were going. We told him we had come from Paris, going to Philippeville. At this he said that we must speak to the governor of Mariembourg. We thought to quiet him as we had done our host at Mézières, saying we were weary and would go the next morning, but he replied, now sharply, that we must follow him at once.

We arose without showing any fear, and speaking quietly in local Bergerac patois, I said to Daniel that once outside, in the dark, we would run for it. We followed the fellow whom we took for the landlord, but who was really a sergeant of the town guard, and saw in the courtyard of the inn, a detachment of eight soldiers with fixed bayonets, at their head the treacherous gamekeeper of Couve. We were immediately seized, and led before the governor, M Pallier by name, who asked us what countrymen we were, and whither we were going. To the first question we told him the truth. To the second I prevaricated, and using my companion's trade, I said we were apprentice hairdressers, out to see France. That our design was to go to Philippeville, from thence to Maubeuge,

Valenciennes, Cambrai, etc., and so return to our own country. The governor had us examined by his valet, who knew something about a barber's work. The valet fortunately began with Daniel, who soon convinced them such was our business.

The governor then asked us of what religion we were. We told him plainly that we were Huguenots, for on this question our conscience would not allow us to disguise the truth. The governor then asked us if our design was not, in reality, to leave the kingdom. This we denied. Alas, may God pardon us that we were weak and foolish enough not to tell the whole truth. But such is human nature, which never performs a good work perfectly.

After the examination, which lasted a good hour, the governor ordered a major who was present to conduct us to prison. This he did, using the same escort and accompanied by the gamekeeper. On the way, the major, named M de La Salle, asked me if it were true that we were from Bergerac. I told him it was.

'I was born about a mile and a half from there,' said he, and asked my family name, on hearing it, exclaiming, 'Why your father is a good friend of mine! Be comforted my children,' he added, 'I will get you out of this unhappy affair. You will be free after two or three days.'

We arrived at the prison, and now the gamekeeper asked the major to have us searched, that he might have his reward, believing we had a great deal of money. We said we had only about one pistole. This the major told us to give to him, whereby we would not be searched. He feared lest we had more about us, which would be taken as a sign we wished to escape from the kingdom, it being well known wandering apprentices are not overburdened with cash. We gave the major our little money, which he said he would remit later to the governor. The gamekeeper, seeing this, had the impudence to tell the major that 'this was not the way Huguenots are to be treated when they flee to Holland,' and attempted to search us himself.

'Rascal!' said the major. 'Do you think to teach me my duty? Leave now, or I'll have you well thrashed.' Such was the only reward this wretch received for the trouble he had taken in causing us to be arrested. Added to which, a few days after, the Prince of Liège, at the solicitation of the Dutch governor of the castle of Couve, dismissed him from his service, and banished him from his dominions, on account of this wicked and treacherous action. Fit wages for such a fellow.

Placed in a cold, dark dungeon, we asked, with tears in our eyes, 'What crime have we committed, sir, that we should be treated as criminals who have deserved the gallows and the wheel?'

'These are my orders for the moment,' said the major, 'but I will take care you don't sleep here!' He went immediately to the governor, telling him that though we had been strictly searched, we had only one pistole on us, proving we had no design of leaving France. And he thought it would be only just and right to set us free. Unfortunately, it was the evening on which the courier left for Paris with the mail, and while we were en route to prison, the governor had written to the court about our detention, and could not now liberate us without its permission. The major entreated the governor at least to release us from the dungeon, and grant us the gaoler's house for our prison, adding he would place a sentinel at the gates to watch us, and that he would be responsible, even if it cost him his head, that we did not escape.

The governor acquiesced, and we had not been an hour in the dungeon, when the major returned with orders that we were to have full liberty within the gaoler's house. He then gave the little money which we had given him to the gaoler, ordering the man to provide us with food as long as the money lasted, as he did not wish that we should appear to be criminals fed by the government.

Meanwhile, at the court, the declaration we had made that we were Huguenots so prejudiced the Marquis de La Vrillière,[31] minister of state, that he would pay no attention to our assurances that we had no intention of leaving the kingdom, and ordered the governor of Mariembourg to prosecute us, and condemn us to the galleys for being found on the frontiers without a passport. Simultaneously, the local priest at Mariembourg was to use every effort to bring us within the Roman Catholic church. If he succeeded we might,

by the favour of the court, be set free to return to
Bergerac. The major read these instructions to us,
adding, 'I give you no advice what to do; faith and
conscience must decide you. All that I can say is that
renouncing your religion will at once open the door of
this prison. If not, you will certainly go to the galleys.'
We replied that we placed our confidence in God and
the principles of our Huguenot religion – not through
obstinacy, but through a firm conviction of the goodness
of our cause. This good major, in his heart a Protestant
like ourselves, though outwardly a Roman Catholic,
embraced us, and left us entreating us not to think it
unkind if he did not see us again.

Our pistole was now exhausted, but they gave us a
pound and a half of bread every day, called 'the King's
bread', while the governor and major, by turns, sent us
food and drink. The priest, who hoped to convert us,
and the nuns of a convent also, sent us occasionally
things to eat, and we, in our turn, fed the gaoler and his
family. This priest came to visit us nearly every day, one
day accompanied by his young and beautiful niece,
whom he brought under the pretext of a charitable visit.
He promised her to me in marriage, with a large dowry,
if I would but turn Catholic. I rejected his offer with
contempt, which so greatly enraged him he declared at
once to the governor and the judge that he had no
longer any hope of our conversion; and that we were
under the influence of the devil. Upon this deposition,

it was resolved to commit us for trial. The judge and his registrar came to interrogate us in the prison, and two days after our sentence was read to us, the substance of which was as follows:

> That being found upon the frontier without passports, and that being of the pretended reformed religion, we were suspected and convicted of having intent to escape from the kingdom, against the ordinances of the King, who has forbidden it; and, as a punishment, we were therefore condemned to be taken to His Majesty's galleys, to remain there in penal servitude for life, with confiscation of our property, etc.

Afterwards, the judge asked us if we wished to appeal to the parliament of Tournay,[32] in the jurisdiction of which the town of Mariembourg is situated. We replied that we would only appeal to God from this iniquitous sentence.

'Do not, I pray you,' said he, 'blame me for the rigour of your sentence; these are the King's orders which condemn you.'

'Sir,' said I, 'the King does not know that I am only *suspected* of intending to leave the kingdom; all that is known is that I am a Protestant. One is not sent to the galleys for being a Huguenot, only for a conviction of the intention of escaping from the kingdom. But you, sir, introduced into the evidence that we were both *suspected* and *convicted* of intending to escape from the kingdom! Not only without proof, but without even examining us to see if there was any proof.'

'What would you have?' said he. 'It is a formality required to obey the King's orders.'

'No longer call yourself a judge, then,' said I, 'but simply an executor of the King's orders.'

'Appeal to the parliament,' said he.

'The parliament will not examine proofs in our favour any more than you,' I told him.

'Very well,' said he, 'I will appeal for you.' We knew this before, as no inferior judge can carry into execution a sentence which involves corporal punishment, without its being ratified by parliament.

'Therefore prepare,' he continued, 'to start for Tournay.'

'We are ready,' we replied.

2. The prisons at Tournay and Lille

THEY SHUT US UP again in the dungeon, and we only left it to set out for Tournay, with four archers, who put fetters on our hands, and bound us together with cords. Our journey was on foot, and very painful. We went by Philippeville, Maubeuge, Valenciennes, and thence to Tournay. Every evening they placed us in the worst dungeons they could find, giving us only bread and water, and neither bed nor straw to rest on.

At Tournay we were confined in the prison of the Parliament. We had not a sou; and as no charitable person entered this prison, as is the custom in many gaols, we became so thin and exhausted that we could no longer stand, and were obliged to lie upon a little damp straw, filled with vermin, close to the door of our cell. Through a hole in this door, our daily ration of bread was thrown to us, as if we were dogs. If we had stayed farther away from the door we should not have had the strength to go and take it.

In this extremity, we sold to the turnkey, for a little bread, our coats and waistcoats, as well as a few shirts we had – only reserving the one which we wore, which

soon fell to rags. We saw no one but the local curé, who
sometimes paid us a visit – but rather to mock, than to
show any compassion, asking if we were not weary of
suffering thus, while repeating our deliverance depen-
ded upon ourselves and our renouncing the errors of
Calvin, discourses so wearisome we did not deign to
answer him.

Such was our situation in the prison of Tournay for
nearly six weeks. Then, one morning about nine o'clock,
the gaoler threw a broom through the door, telling us
to sweep out our dungeon as they were about to bring
in two gentlemen to keep us company. We asked of what
they were accused.

'Huguenots,' said he, 'like you.'

A quarter of an hour afterwards the cell door opened,
and the gaoler, together with some armed soldiers, led
in two young gentlemen covered with lace from head to
foot whom we recognised as fellow-townsmen of
Bergerac, sons of well-to-do citizens, with whom we
had once been schoolfellows. They, understandably,
did not recognise us. As soon as the escort shut the
door, we saluted them by name – Sorbier, and Rivasson.
They pretended to be nobles: Sorbier called himself
'Chevalier', and Rivasson, 'Marquis', titles they had
assumed to facilitate their escape from France, and
thinking we had been put in the cell to trick them, they
refused to answer to their own names. At this, we then
addressed them in the patois of Bergerac, they inquired

who we were, and we told them our names. They, much
astonished, told us that our relatives and friends, having
heard nothing for six or seven months, believed us to
be dead. Indeed, since our detention we had not been
allowed to write. We all embraced, shedding tears at the
sad situation in which we found ourselves, when these
gentlemen asked us if we had anything to eat, being
very hungry. We gave them our wretched morsel of
bread, intended for the whole day; and our pitcher of
water.

'Good God!' they cried, and asked if food could be
bought.

'Certainly,' said I, 'But only for coin.'

'Oh!' said they, 'If it's only money . . .' They cut the
seams of their belts and trousers, and the soles of their
shoes, and nearly four hundred louis d'or fell out. I
confess that I never felt greater joy than at the sight of
that gold. One of them gave me a coin, and I knocked
with all my strength at the door. The gaoler came and
asked us what we wanted.

'To eat!' I said, showing him the louis d'or.

'Very well, gentlemen,' said he, 'What will it be?
Soup and boiled beef?'

'Yes,' said I, 'A good thick soup, a ten pound loaf,
and some beer.'

'An hour,' said he.

'An hour!' I exclaimed – the two gentlemen laughing
at my eagerness.

At last they brought us a thick cabbage soup, a dish of boiled beef, and a ten pound loaf. The two gentlemen ate very little; but Daniel and myself fell upon the soup in such a ravenous manner that, having so long been accustomed to a spare diet, I suffered greatly, and an apothecary had to be sent for to administer an emetic. When I had recovered, I told them all which had passed with us since our departure from Bergerac, and that possibly the galleys awaited all of us. At this, they began to weep, confessing that they had resolved to renounce their religion rather than be condemned to the galleys.

'What an example, gentlemen,' said I, 'you bring us here! We should wish rather never to have seen you than to find you holding sentiments so opposed to the education which your parents gave you. And to the faith in which you have been instructed. Do you not tremble of the just judgment of God?'

'What would you have us do?' they replied. 'We cannot go to the galleys. We praise you in having courage to do so, but our resolution is taken.'

We could do nothing but pray God to bring them to a better mind. Even so, their money had prevented us from dying of hunger, and as their release grew nearer, fear of starvation made me supplicate with clasped hands that they might leave us three or four gold louis, telling them I would write an order that my father would honour at Bergerac where they said they would be going to give him news of us. But they were so hard-hearted that, on leaving, they would only give us half a louis. Even that was not to be spent in this prison, for we were almost immediately transferred to the prison of the town, named Le Beffroi, rather than that of the parliament where we had lain up to now. Here we were very much better off than in that of the parliament prison. We were allowed to write home, and many Protestants, respectable citizens of Tournay, had permission to visit us. They 'greased the paw', as the expression is, of the gaoler, who at their solicitation opened our cell door every morning that we might take the air in a small courtyard close by, where our zealous friends would console us as much as they could, and exhort us to perseverance.

Some time after, a councillor came to see us, and told us that we had been very strongly recommended to him, and that he would see if he could not rescue us from our sad plight. We could not imagine whence came this recommendation, unless our parents, to whom we had written, had procured it through persons of considera-tion among their friends. This councillor remained a good hour with us, asking questions about our route, where we been arrested, and in what way. He made us repeat the occurrence at Couve, and he asked us if we could prove that we had lodged at an inn in that town.

We replied that nothing was easier than to verify it, upon which he said, 'Take courage, my lads. Tomorrow I will send a lawyer, who will give you a requisition to

sign; and you will see its effects!' Next day the lawyer
duly arrived, and read to us the requisition he had
drawn up, and which we signed. This was to the effect,
that simply being Huguenots did not warrant the
punishment which the law pronounces against all who
try to escape from France; and that we would prove we
were not escaping from the kingdom, because we had
already left it once – having passed through Couve,
which was outside the kingdom – but chose ourselves to
once more to return to France; that Couve was a town
of the Prince of Liège, with a Dutch garrison, under the
protection of which we could at once have placed
ourselves in absolute safety. This signed requisition was
then tabled in the criminal court of the parliament for
all to examine.

Two days afterwards, three huissiers[33] came to take
us before the president. He, showing us the document,
asked if we had signed and presented it. We replied that
we had, and that we prayed the venerable assembly to
regard it favourably. The president said that they had
examined it, and said the first thing we had to prove
was that we knew Couve was outside the French
territories. This was a question we had not expected,
but replied boldly enough, and without hesitation, we
knew it perfectly well.

'How?' said he. 'Two young lads who have never left
their firesides, while Couve is more than six hundred
miles from your home.' I did not know how to reply, but

my companion at once said that he knew it before he left Bergerac, because, having served as a barber in a company of the regiment of Picardy, he had witnessed the arranging of the boundaries in that part of the country.

'So you were in, and then left, the service?' asked the president.

'Yes.'

'And so have your discharge?'

Daniel, taking out his pocketbook, produced the said discharge. The president sent it round among the assembly. It was then attached it to the requisition, and we were taken back to prison. Two hours later, the gaoler ran into our cell to congratulate us upon our approaching deliverance. A clerk of the parliament had told him, having seen with his own eyes the resolution of the assembly, to fully absolve us from the accusation of attempting to escape from the kingdom. Our good friends of the town at once came in crowds to congratulate us, and we expected our release every hour.

We were then informed that though it was true that the parliament had acquitted us, we were state criminals, and therefore could not be set free without the orders of the court. So the Marquis de La Vrillière, minister of state, had been written to, to acquaint him we had perfectly proved our innocence. And that all that was awaited now was his orders as to our dispensation. The minister replied to be careful that the proofs were sound, to examine them well. The parliament, unwilling to contradict itself, wrote back that the proofs were complete. A fortnight passed and the final orders of the court arrived. We were summoned before the full assembly. The president asked if we could read, and on our replying in the affirmative, he said, giving us the letter of the Marquis de La Vrillière, 'Read this, then.'

Owing to its brevity, I have remembered its exact words, as follows:

Gentlemen,

Jean Marteilhe, Daniel Le Gras, having been found upon the frontiers without passports, His Majesty decides that they shall be condemned to the galleys.

I am, gentlemen, etc.,
The Marquis de La Vrillière.'

'Here, my friends,' said the president and several of his councillors, 'is your sentence, which has emanated from the court, and not from us; we wash our hands of it. We pity you, and we wish you the mercy of God, and of the King.'

We were taken back to Le Beffroi, and the same evening a councillor and registrar of the parliament came to the prison. Having made us enter the gaoler's room, the councillor told us to 'kneel before God and the law and to listen to the official reading of the sentence.' We obeyed. The substance, after the preamble, being simply:

> The said Jean Marteilhe and Daniel Le Gras having been suspected and convicted of professing the pretended reformed religion, and of attempting to escape from the kingdom in order to profess freely the said religion, for punishment of which crime, we condemn them to serve as convicts in the King's galleys, for life, . . . etc.

After the councillor finished, I said, 'How, sir, can such a just and venerable body as the parliament make this sentence agree with your decision to acquit us?'

'The parliament,' said he, 'acquitted you, but the court, which is superior to parliaments, condemns you.'

'But where, sir, is justice, which ought to direct both tribunals?'

'It is not for you,' said he 'to fathom these things.'

I then begged the councillor to give us an authentic copy of our sentence, which he did. Three days later, the archers of the grand provost came for us, and after we had been bound and fettered in irons, we set off for Lille, in Flanders, where one of the 'chains' of galley slaves assembled.

We arrived at Lille in the evening, much exhausted with walking fifteen miles in irons, and were immediately taken us to the town prison. As the chief gaoler searched us, either by chance or design, there were two Jesuit fathers present. They took our books of devotion and my copy of the sentence, and I overheard one say to the other, that it was a great imprudence of the parliament to give authentic copies of such documents. I never again saw the books or the sentence.

After this, we were taken to the Tower of St Pierre, especially set apart for galley slaves, on account of the thickness of its walls. Inside, we were thrown in the dungeon of the galley slaves – one of the most frightful dens I have ever seen. It was spacious, but so dark that the unfortunates there never know whether it is day or night, except by the bread and water which is issued every morning. What is worse, neither fire nor light was allowed. One had to lie down upon a little straw that had been torn and gnawed by rats and mice, of which there were great numbers; and who ate with impunity our bread, because we could not see to drive them away. In this dungeon were about thirty villains of every kind, condemned for divers crimes, whose first act was to demand money under the penalty of tossing us in a counterpane. Rather than experience this we gave them two crowns, an amount they taxed us without mercy.

About two days later, a wretched newcomer, through want of money rather than of courage, had to endure what we escaped. The method was this. They stretched their victim on an old counterpane of coarse cloth; then four of the most robust each took a corner, and raising it as high as they could, let it fall down upon the stone floor of the cell; as many times as the poor wretch's sentence had been decreed in years. This horrible punishment made me shudder. The miserable victim had good reason to cry out, but there was no compassion. The gaoler, to whom all the money which this execrable game produces goes in the end, did nothing but laugh. He looked through the hole in the door, crying to the victim, 'Courage, comrade!' The poor wretch was so bruised by his repeated falls that they thought he would have died. Nevertheless, he recovered.

A few days after, I, in my turn, underwent an equally terrible experience. Every evening, the gaoler, accompanied by four great rogues of turnkeys, and the guard of the prison, visited the dungeon to see if any were making attempts to escape, examining carefully the walls and the floor. All these men, to the number of about twenty, were armed with pistols, swords, and bayonets. One evening, after they had paid their visit, and were retiring, and as the last turnkey was locking the door, I addressed a few words to him. He answered me amiably enough, and thinking I had conciliated him, I asked him for the bit of candle which he held in his hand, that we might rid ourselves of the vermin which so tormented us. He shut the door in my face and I remarked aloud, not thinking he was near enough to hear me, that I was sorry I had not snatched the candle from his hand.

The next morning, when our fellow prisoners were

awake and singing their Catholic litanies (otherwise the priests would give them no alms) and I was sleeping on my bit of straw, I was suddenly awakened by several blows from the flat side of a sword. I started up and saw the gaoler, sword in hand, the four turnkeys, and all the soldiers of the guard, armed to the teeth. I asked them why they ill-treated me thus. The gaoler only replied by giving me twenty more blows, while the turnkey with the candle-end gave me such a terrible box in the ear that he knocked me down. Having got up again, the gaoler told me to follow him. Perceiving that it was to do me more injury, I refused to obey, until I knew by whose orders he treated me thus, for I believed the grand provost alone could order me to be punished. At this they beat me until I fell down a second time.

The four turnkeys now took me up, two by the legs and two by the arms, and carried me out of the dungeon, dragging me like a dead dog down the steps of the tower into the courtyard, where they opened the door of a stone staircase which led underground. Pushing me down the steps, about twenty-five or thirty, at the bottom they opened a cell with an iron gate, called the 'dungeon of the sorceress', forced me in, shut the door, and went away. Being able to see no more than if I had my eyes shut, I groped a few steps to find a little straw, and found myself up to knees in water as cold as ice. I turned back and leaned against the door, where the ground was higher and less damp. I did find a little straw upon which to sit, but had not been there two minutes, when I felt the water coming through. I firmly believed that they had buried me alive, and felt that that dungeon would be my tomb if I remained there twenty-four hours.

Half an hour after, the turnkey brought me some bread and water. I rejected this, saying, 'Go tell your butcher of a master that I will neither eat nor drink, till I have spoken to the grand provost.' The turnkey went away, and in less than an hour the gaoler came alone with a candle in his hand, armed with nothing but a bunch of keys. Opening the door, he told me, quite kindly, to follow him upstairs. Dirty, covered with blood from my nose and head, he led me into his kitchen and washing off the blood, put a plaster on my bruises. He gave me a glass of Canary wine, and reprimanding me slightly for my imprudence about the turnkey's candle, we had breakfast together.

After, he led me into a cell in the courtyard which was dry and light, as, he said, he could not put me back with the other galley slaves after what had happened. I remained four or five days in this cell, during which time the gaoler sent me my dinner from his table. Next, he proposed to place my comrade, Daniel, and myself, in a chamber in the prison where there was a good bed and every necessary comfort, for two louis d'or a month. As we were not well provided with money I offered him a louis and a half up to the time when the chain started. He refused, but a few days later I was placed in a large room, with a comfortable bed, and well-fed without its costing me anything. I saw that he wished to oblige us to give him the two louis a month, but, reckoning our purse, and considering that if the chain did not start for two or three months, we could by no means afford it, I kept strictly to my initial offer. At this, he put me back into the tower. Daniel, who had thought me lost, was delighted to feel me near him. I say feel, for we could not see, we had no light for that.

One morning, about nine o'clock, the gaoler opened our dungeon, and calling my companion and myself, told us to follow him. We thought that he was going to put us into the chamber for one louis and a half, but once out of the dungeon he said, 'It is M Lambertie, grand provost of Flanders, and grand master here, who wishes to speak with you. I hope,' continued he, 'you will tell him nothing about what happened recently.'

'When I have pardoned,' said I, 'I forget, and do not seek revenge.'

We arrived at an apartment where we found M de Lambertie, who gave us a most gracious reception. He held in his hand a letter from his brother, a gentleman of Protestant origin, who lived three leagues from Bergerac. My father had procured this recommendation for us. M de Lambertie began by saying how sorry he was not to be able to obtain our release.

'For any other crime,' said he, 'I should have

sufficient influence at court. But all that I can do in this case is to try to make you comfortable, and to keep you here as long as I can, though the chain is just starting for the galleys.' He then asked the gaoler what comfortable chambers were empty. The gaoler mentioned two or three which M de Lambertie rejected, saying, 'I not only desire that these gentlemen have every comfort, but, also, that they enjoy some recreation. Therefore, place them in the alms room.'

'But, sir,' said the gaoler, 'that room has only civil prisoners, with liberties I dare not give condemned criminals.'

'Well,' replied M Lambertie, 'I command that you give those liberties! And good beds! And all they desire for their comfort, putting it to my account! And do not take a sou from them. Although remember it is your business to take care that they do not escape! Gentlemen,' he said to us, 'this alms room is the largest and most cheerful in the whole prison. And, besides costing you nothing, you can make some money there. I order,' he then said to the gaoler, 'that you make M Marteilhe provost of that room.'

We thanked M de Lambertie for his great kindness, and he told us that he would often come to the prison to ensure the gaoler performed his orders with respect to us, and then retired. We were placed in the alms room, where I was installed provost, to the great regret of my predecessor, who was moved elsewhere. The alms room was very large, and contained six beds of twelve civil prisoners, generally people of some respectability. Besides these, were one or two young scapegraces, pickpockets, or prisoners for some light offences, whose business it was to make the beds, to cook, and keep the room clean. These latter slept upon a mattress in a corner of the apartment. They were, in fact, our servants.

The provostship of the alms room means that he who possesses this office has to distribute all the charitable donations made to the prison. There is a box which hangs by a chain from the sill of the window to receive the charity of the passers by. These alms are generally considerable, and are all brought into this room to the provost, who has the key of this box, and opens it every evening to distribute the money to all the prisoners – both civil (if they wish it) and criminal. Besides this, every morning, the turnkeys go with carts or barrows throughout the town to collect the offerings of bakers, butchers, brewers, and fishmongers; and also to all the different markets, all they collect being brought to the alms room, again to be distributed throughout all the apartments and cells by the provost, in proportion to the number of prisoners in each, of which the gaoler gives him a list every day. And of which the total when I was there was from five to six hundred. The gaoler received his share from the box, to use it, he said, in making soup. But what soup that was! Bad and putrid pieces of beef, cooked with water and a little salt, the very smell of which made me sick. But although I had become the distributor-general of these alms, I was unable to remedy one abuse. This was the prevention any charities reaching those condemned to the galleys.

After six happy weeks, M de Lambertie told us that a chain was to start tomorrow for Dunkirk, where there were six of the King's galleys stationed. But that he exempted us from going, passing us off for sick, but we must remain in bed till the chain had started. This we did, and procured the blessing of another three months in comfort.

3. To Dunkirk in the galley chain 1702

IN JANUARY 1702, M de Lambertie came to see us, to tell us another chain would start the next day, and that he could still procure our exemption from it, but that he must warn us that this would be the last which would be going to the Dunkirk galleys, all subsequent ones would go to Marseilles, a journey of more than nine hundred miles, which we should be obliged to walk on foot, linked together by fetters round our necks. Moreover, since he himself was committed to going into the country in March he would no longer be able to render us any useful service. He therefore advised us to start next day to Dunkirk – the chain would be under his orders as far as that town, and he would arrange to have us sent in a cart, apart from the other galley slaves, the distance being about thirty-five miles.

After a discussion we adopted his suggestion, and this good nobleman kept his word: for, instead of being chained to the twenty-five or thirty prisoners who composed the band, and who went on foot, we went by cart, with a good bed provided every evening, and to the extent that the officer of the archers who guarded the chain had us take our meals at his table, whereby we were taken for people of great distinction. But this comfort was only smoke which soon disappeared. For the third day after our departure from Lille, we arrived at Dunkirk, and were placed in the galley *L'Heureuse*, under Captain de La Pailleterie, who was head of the squadron of the six galleys at present at Dunkirk. And here, on *L'Heureuse*, as they put us each on separate benches, in different galleys, I was finally parted from my dear companion, Daniel Le Gras. From these temporary galleys we would be distributed to the final vessels chosen for us.

We had heard much of the terrible punishment of the bastinado and the very day of our arrival, we saw it administered to an unfortunate convict, for what offence I know not. I was terrified at witnessing this punishment, which takes place without any form of trial, and usually immediately. The manner of its infliction is as follows: the unfortunate victim is stripped naked from his waist upwards; then they make him lie upon his face, his legs hanging over his bench, and his arms over the bench opposite. Two convicts hold his legs and two others his arms, his back is bare and exposed. There is a comite, or overseer, present, and also a galley slave, usually a muscular Turk, also stripped, who will administer the punishment. There is also the major of the galleys who must always be present at such punishments. The comite stands behind the Turk and every now and then strikes him with a whip, to urge him on to greater efforts in scourging the back of the victim, which is done with a coarse thick rope. As the Turk knows that there will be no mercy for him if he spares the victim, he applies his blows with his whole force, so that each stroke raises a bruise an inch in height. Those who suffer this punishment can rarely endure more than ten or twelve blows without losing the power of speech and motion. This does not hinder the number of strokes to a body which neither moves, nor utters a cry, till the sentence is accomplished. Twenty or thirty blows are given for slight offences; while I have seen fifty, eighty, and even a hundred given. In such cases the victims scarcely ever recover. After the appointed number, the barber or surgeon of the galley rubs the victim's lacerated back with strong vinegar and salt, to make the body regain its sensibility, and to prevent gangrene. Such is the bastinado of the galleys.

Imagine my horror next day when I almost received the same treatment, through the malice of a great rascal of a convict who was at the galleys for robbery. First he insulted me, to which I replied not a word, and then asked for money, having seen me pay for five or six bottles of wine for those on my bench. To this I replied that I only gave money to those who did not ask for it. This wretch, named Poulet, then told the sous-comite of the galley, that I had uttered terrible blasphemies against the Virgin Mary and all the saints of Paradise. The sous-comite, a brutal barbarian, as are all his class, told me to strip at once to receive the bastinado. One can judge of my emotions, knowing I had neither said nor done anything to warrant this punishment. I asked my companions on the bench why they were going to treat me thus: if it was the custom to make all newcomers pass this ordeal. They seemed as surprised as I.

The sous-comite began down the gangplank to alert the major of the galleys. On the way down he met the first comite of the galley, informing him of my supposed horrible blasphemies against the Blessed Virgin, and all the saints. The comite asked him if he had heard these blasphemies himself. No; the convict Poulet had given him the information. The comite was tolerably honest, and very serious for a man of his profession. He came up to my bench and asked me what reason I had had to blaspheme against the Catholic religion. I replied I had never done so, and that my own religion forbade such a thing. At this, the comite called Poulet, asking what I had said and done. This rogue had the impudence to repeat the same things. The comite then questioned the six slaves on my bench, and those on benches before and behind. Twenty to twenty-eight persons all testified I had never uttered a word, good or bad; that I had merely told Poulet I would not treat those who asked me to do so. At this, the comite severely belaboured Poulet, had him bound with a double chain to the criminal bench, and strongly reprimanded his sous-comite.

As with the rest of mankind, there are some comites who are more malicious and cruel than others, one of whom, in the next galley along, *La Palme*, was said to be a very demon. He always had the bourrasque, or cleaning-out of his galley, done every day, instead of every Saturday, as all others did. During this exercise, lasting two or three hours, the strokes from the whips of the overseers fell on the slaves like hail, the other convicts on my bench constantly saying to me, 'Pray God in the distribution you may not fall to *La Palme*!'

After a fortnight, this redistribution arrived. First we were examined in the arsenal and divided into classes, the strongest and the weakest mixed together. Six lots were made, and the six comites (although I did not know them to be so) drew for us. They had placed me in the first class, at the head of a lot. The comite to whom my lot fell told us to follow him to his galley. Curious to know my fate, and ignorant that this man was *the* comite, I prayed him to tell me to what galley I had fallen.

'*La Palme*,' said he. I made an exclamation deploring my bad fortune. 'Why,' said he, 'are you more unfortunate than the others?'

'Because, sir,' said I, 'I have fallen to a galley whose comite is a perfect fiend.' He looked at me with a frown.

'If I knew,' said he, 'who told you that, they would

soon repent it.' I saw I had said too much, and there was no remedy. However, after leading us aboard, he at once showed a mark of his favour toward me. For as I was young and strong, the argousin, an under-officer charged with guarding the galley slaves, had put round my leg an iron ring and a chain of excessive weight and thickness.

The comite perceived this, and, with a rude and brutal air, said to this argousin, that if he did not take off the chain he would complain to the captain. He would not allow his best subject for wielding an oar to be spoiled. The argousin at once took off the chain, replacing it with one of the lightest which the comite chose himself – fastening me to his (the comite's) own bench. I must mention that the comite eats and sleeps on a bench of the galley, upon which a table standing on four little iron pillars is erected. This table is both long enough for him to take his meals at; and also to spread his bed upon, surrounded by a tent of coarse cotton cloth. This means the convicts of this bench are under the table, which can easily be removed when they want to row or perform manoeuvres. The six convicts of this bench compose the domestic establishment of the comite. Each has his special employment, and when the comite takes his meals, or is seated on his table, all the convicts of this bench, and those on either side, stand with heads uncovered.

It is the great ambition of all the convicts in the galley

to be on the bench of the comite or sous-comite, not only because they are allowed the remnants of their meals, but principally because these slaves never receive any strokes of the lash. These benches are called 'the reserved seats'. I, then, had the privilege of being on this bench, but it did not last long. This was through my own fault, for, full of the remains of worldly pride, I would not dance attendance as the others did – and when the comite was at table I would lay down, or turned my back upon him, my cap on my head, pretending to look at the sea, contenting myself with being the slave of the King, without being that of the comite as well. In this I ran a great risk.

The comite, however, demon as he had been painted, was very reasonable. He inquired of the convicts of his bench if I ate with them the remains of his meals. Hearing that I would never taste them, he said, 'He has not forgotten his former good living; leave him alone.' One evening, after he had gone to bed in his tent, he called me to him. Speaking in a whisper, he told me that he saw I had not been brought up as a vagabond, in that I would not submit to cringe to him like the others. He added he did not esteem me less for it, but must make me an example by sending me to another bench. But that I might reckon, on never receiving a blow from him or his under-comites.

I thanked him for his kindness, and can truly say that he kept his word, which, with him, was a great thing.

For while we were rowing or making manoeuvres, he would not have regarded his own father, and would have whipped him as any one else. He was the cruellest man, in the exercise of his authority, I have ever seen but, when not in a passion, both reasonable and just in his judgment. There were five Huguenots in his galley, none of whom ever received the least ill-treatment from him.

It was otherwise with the galley captain, the Chevalier de Langeron Maulévrier,[34] who hated us extremely, and, when we were rowing, with our bodies naked, as was the custom, would call to the comite, 'Refresh the backs of those Huguenots with a salad of whip strokes.' But these blows always fell upon someone else – possibly through the interest of M Piecourt, a rich and celebrated banker. For it must be known that the Protestant brethren of the French churches in the Netherlands sent remittances to their brethren suffering in the galleys of France. This money generally passed through Amsterdam, whence a banker sent it to an agent in the places where the galleys were. And here, in Dunkirk, this agent was M Piecourt, a native of Bordeaux and a Protestant by birth and at heart, but outwardly a Papist. From Amsterdam, one of my relations, an elder of the Walloon Church, charged that I should receive the money from M Piecourt, and distribute it among the Huguenots of the Dunkirk galleys. I accepted, though this office is a very perilous one. For, if you are found out, you risk being bastinadoed to death, unless you reveal the name of the banker from whom you had the money, when the banker would be utterly ruined.

The Jesuits, who have always persecuted us to the utmost, and never found any opportunity of increasing suffering which they did not embrace with ardour, knew we were being sent this money. They reasoned that if this resource was stopped, hunger could be used to try to convert us. So they proposed to the court that it issue orders to the galley-masters at Marseilles and Dunkirk to have a close watch kept for any remitting money to the slaves. The court did not fail to send these orders, commanding they be carried out with rigour. Now the greatest attention began to be given to find out what bankers or merchants furnished the money.

Although I was commissioned to receive these remittances, I was chained to my bench, without having the liberty to go into the town. This was through the malice of the chaplain of the galleys, who prevents us from having this privilege, although it is granted to convicts condemned for secular crimes – who merely pay a sou to the argousin and a sou to the guard who accompanies them. How, then, was I to receive this money? M Piecourt initially sent it by his clerk. But with the new threats, M Piecourt's clerk no longer dared thus to expose himself, and M Piecourt begged me to find someone of fidelity whom I could send to collect the money.

I opened my heart to the Turk on my bench, Isouf,

who joyfully undertook to render me this service, putting his hand upon his turban, which is with them the sign of the outpouring of the heart to God, and thanking him with all his soul for the favour which he had shown him in giving him the opportunity to exercise charity, even at the peril of his blood, for Isouf knew well enough that if taken, he would be bastinadoed to death to make him reveal what banker had paid over the money. Isouf served me in this way very faithfully for several years, without ever accepting the smallest reward from me, alleging that if he did so he would cancel all his good deeds.

Of course, M Piecourt, through being solicited in my favour from people whose goodwill he valued, therefore thought I was worth the trouble of any service he might be able to offer. And his purse, therefore, was always open to oblige the great nobles, by whom he was much caressed and flattered. He had already spoken on my behalf to our captain, the Chevalier de Langeron, who, as he was his great friend, granted me several indul-gences, and one day begged my captain to have the kindness to order that I should be brought to M Piecourt's house the next morning, which was Christmas day, 1701, at eight o'clock. M Piecourt chose this time that his wife might not know; for she was a bigoted Papist, who, that day, would remain in church till noon. In the course of the evening, M de Langeron came to the galley (in winter these gentlemen do not live on board) to order the argousin to take me, next morning, without a chain, to M Piecourt's, and to wait at the street-door, or in the hall, till I had finished my business with him.

Next morning, at eight, M Piecourt told his servants we were not to be disturbed, then, exaggerating the desire to render me any service, stated he had devised a scheme for my release. I thanked him, saying I would do all he directed, provided it reconciled with conscience.

'Conscience,' said he, 'has little to do with it, you will not feel it. But if you do, you can atone when you get to Holland. Listen,' he continued, 'I am a Protestant, like you, but have good reason, on account of my fortune, to play the hypocrite before the world. I don't believe there is any great harm in it, when one does not apostatise at heart. Here, then, is the scheme I've devised. M de Pontchartrain, the minister of marine, is a friend of mine, and will grant me anything. All you have is to sign a declaration in which you promise, if set at liberty, to live and die a good Roman Catholic no matter what country you may be in. There will be no ceremony, and no one will ever know – even among your own brethren. Do this, and I assure you that within a fortnight you shall be released, when I will send you safely over to Holland. What do you think?'

'I think, sir,' replied I, 'that I was deceived in believing you to be a good Protestant. Protestant you may be, but we must take away the word "good". Why, sir! Do you think that God is deaf and blind? And that the promise you wish me to make, though concealed from the eye of man, would not be seen by *Him*? As for the promise itself, I have only to make the same before the chaplain of my galley, and he would at once procure me my release.' I then said I did not think that my relations in Amsterdam would wish him to procure me my release at the expense of my conscience.

'Certainly not,' said he quickly, 'And for my part I prefer they do not know of it.' He then embraced me, with tears in his eyes, telling me, 'I do not love you so much, on account of the recommendations from Amsterdam, but out of pure respect for those excellent sentiments you profess; and I shall watch for every opportunity to render you services.' He then offered me as much money as I needed. I thanked him, took leave, and returned to my galley, after which M Piecourt frequently came to see me, always offering his services to myself, and to the captain. And truly, this captain always needed money, being so magnificent and extravagant that five hundred francs a month which the King gave to each galley captain was not half enough.

The captains have generally for their pantry, which is in the galley hold, a cabin-boy or waiter, an office generally held by a convict, and very sought-after. For he who gets it, is then exempt from rowing, and makes good cheer in the captain's kitchen. Now it happened that Captain de Langeron's waiter had stolen fifty or sixty pounds of coffee, which the steward missed from the store-room, immediately telling the captain who, without any form of trial or examination, at once ordered that fifty strokes of the bastinado to this poor rogue of a waiter, then condemning him to the criminal bench. The captain then ordered the comite to find him an honest waiter from among the convicts. The comite laughed at the word 'honest', but said there was an old slave, named Bancilhon, scarcely capable of rowing, who might do.

'But,' he added, 'I know you will not have him.'

'Why not?' asked the captain'

'Because,' said the comite, 'he is a Huguenot.'

The captain frowned, then asked, 'Is there no other?'

'None I can answer for.'

'Then send him,' said the captain, and as soon as he saw Bancilhon, whose candour and integrity were imprinted on his countenance, he asked if he wished to serve as waiter. The air and prudence with which Bancilhon replied pleased the captain, who had him at once installed in the pantry, and soon became so fond of him that he even entrusted his purse to him. When any money given to him by the captain was spent, Bancilhon would produce the bills for inspection. And so great confidence had the captain in him that he often tore up these memoranda without looking at them, and threw them into the sea.

Obviously, this confidence in Bancilhon, and Bancilhon's honesty and great economy, soon made him four mortal enemies – namely the captain's cook; his purser; and first and second stewards. These four took their meals at the second table, and often wished to supplement them with champagne and other delicacies entrusted to the care of Bancilhon, who refused them, saying such things were only for the captain. They therefore determined to ruin him. They would choose a day when the captain was having a dinner party, all hurry and confusion, and would steal a piece of silver plate (with which the captain was well provided) and then accuse Bancilhon. However, the second steward involved, Moria, either out of goodwill to Bancilhon, or probably to supplant one of his colleagues, told Bancilhon of the plot.

Bancilhon decided not to wait for the storm of their malice, which he knew, sooner or later, would ruin him. Instead, he took the current bills in hand and went to the captain, begging him to instantly discharge him. Much surprised, the captain asked why. Bancilhon pleaded his age, and added his failing memory and sight no longer permitted him to profit by the captain's kindness. The captain said there must be some other reason, which he wished to know immediately under penalty of his anger. Bancilhon then repeated what Moria, the second steward, had told him.

'Call them!' said the captain. They came and he threatened to throw them into the sea, if they did not confess. They did so, begging for pardon a thousand times.

'Well, gentlemen,' said he, 'I shall not impose any other punishment except to declare that from this moment, if anything is missing of which Bancilhon has the charge, you will be held responsible.' Exclaiming that Bancilhon could ruin them at any moment, they retired confused, and never after attempted to supplant Bancilhon, who continued the favourite servant of M de Langeron, whose kindness to him was equally reflected upon us other four Protestants.

In July this same year, 1702, we cruised our six galleys to the fort of Ostend. And from thence, when the sea was calm, along the coast of Blankenbourg and L'Ecluse, in Flanders. Then we returned towards Nieuport, and the entrance of the Ostend Channel. Ostend was a particularly good port for the galleys, as about six miles from the coast was a large sandbank over which large vessels, that draw much water, cannot pass, while galleys can easily do so.

One very calm day, for it must be quite calm for the galleys to proceed to sea, we saw from the heights of Nieuport a squadron of twelve becalmed Dutch vessels of war about fifteen miles away. We rowed out to reconnoitre, and seeing one ship stranded about three miles distant from the others, all six of our galleys began to advance abreast. The captain of this ship, a great simpleton, was not aware that, as galleys are low in the deck at a distance they do not appear to be very large. He therefore said boastingly to his crew, 'Let us prepare to haul these six boats on board.' But his head surgeon, a French refugee named Labadoux who knew the strength of the galleys, told him plainly that if he allowed the galleys to approach his vessel they would take it, owing to the great number of men they carried. Notwithstanding this advice, the captain made no effort to either to prepare his artillery, or to have his vessel towed by his boats to within the safety of the squadron.

We now began to row hard – at the same time making the chamade. This is a cry which galley slaves raise to terrify the enemy. In truth, it is a fearsome sight to see on each of the six galleys three hundred naked men, all rowing in good time and shaking their chains. This, together with their yells and shrieks, make those who have never before witnessed such a thing, shudder in horror. Thus was it with the crew of this ship: too weak to resist, being composed of only one hundred and eighty men. For so frightened were they, they rushed down to the hold of their ship, crying out for quarter. The soldiers and sailors of our galleys had no trouble in boarding and seizing the vessel, called the *Unicorn*, of Rotterdam, fifty-four guns, which we quickly towed off, in sight of the other ships who could not follow us for want of wind, and brought her into Ostend. We made no other expedition during the remainder of the campaign, and then returned in October to dismantle and winter at Dunkirk.

4. Incidents at the galleys, Dunkirk 1703-1705

THE YEAR 1703 passed without our doing anything but alarming the English coast by cruising the Channel firing cannon-shots, and this only when the weather permitted it. In the year 1704 we were at Ostend, watching another Dutch squadron which cruised off the harbour, and when it was calm rowing out and worrying them by firing heavy cannon at them, our range being greater than that of their guns, returning to Ostend whenever a little breeze arose.

One day, the Dutch admiral, Almonde,[35] was cruising with six men-of-war off Blankenbourg, north of Ostend, when a fisherman of that coast came aboard to sell his catch. Almonde bribed the fisherman to come in to Ostend, and tell our commander of the galleys that he had just met six large Dutch vessels, returning from the East Indies, so heavily laden with treasure, and their crews so ill with scurvy, that they could scarcely work the ships. Then adding he had been on board these vessels and seen for himself while making a good thing of selling all his fish to them. As one easily believes what one wishes, our commander fell into the trap, and, as the tide flowed, about ten in the evening, our six galleys put to sea for these rich prizes.

We rowed all night, and at daybreak we saw what we believed to be our six Dutch East-Indiamen. These, immediately they perceived us, pretended to put on all sail, and moved into file, ahead and astern, one after the other. So that we, coming up from the rear, could discern little about them. They were well camouflaged, their stern ornaments covered up, their gunports closed, their topsails lowered – to all the world slow, rich, merchant vessels returning from a long voyage. All our officers, sailors, and soldiers, felt nothing but joy, in the firm hope of a great prize of gold, silks and spices.

As we continued to advance, they put up a little more sail to make us believe that they were afraid, and to draw us more surely within range of their guns. But although they seemed to crowd on sail, they found means not to advance by dragging a large double cable behind their ships. We, for our parts, rowed with all our might, thinking that the Indiamen were so heavy with booty that they could not make way. Coming in range, we fired at them. In reply, their rearguard replied by firing a small cannon which did not reach half way to us, and which encouraged us even more. So we advanced recklessly, pouring a terrible fire from our artillery, until, at last, we found ourselves so near to the rear ship that we prepared to board it, axes and sabres in hand.

At which their admiral made a signal, and all their fleet veered round; and in a moment, we were surrounded by these five great ships, who, letting down their gunports, poured upon us a terrible fire, cutting away the greater portion of our masts and rigging, and made great slaughter among our crews. Perceiving his mistake, our commander gave the signal for instant flight towards the sandbank, which our enemies could not prevent us from reaching. But they escorted us thither with such terrible fire that we ran the greatest peril in the world of being all sunk. At last we were safe behind the sandbank, but with more than two hundred and fifty men killed, and many more wounded.

Arrived at Ostend, the first thing to be done was to seek for the fisherman who had betrayed us, who, had he been found, would have been hanged immediately, but he had not been foolish enough to wait for us. Everybody spoke of our commander's credulity and imprudence in risking the loss to the King of six galleys of three thousand souls (for these galleys have five hundred men each). I say his imprudence, for one of the captains, M de Fontete, had strongly suspected that it might be a trick, and said he thought it would be well to make sure by sending our brigantine to reconnoitre the fleet. But the commander telling him it was fear of the cannon shots which made him think so, M de Fontete replied without hesitation, 'Then let us attack the enemy at once, and you will see if I am afraid.'

Words which cost us a great deal of blood, for when our commander gave the signal to retreat, M de Fontete, stung with his previous reproach, acted as if he had not seen it. Our commander, now having retired with the other five galleys to the sandbank, and seeing M de Fontete's galley now in the thick of the action, exclaimed, 'So! Fontete wishes to challenge me to be as brave as he is, does he! Come,' said he to his comite, 'row up again to the enemy.'

The comite, foreseeing his own death, fell on his knees, entreating him not to go, but the commander, pistol in hand, threatened to kill him if he did not execute his orders immediately. The comite obeyed, and rowing out again to take the order to M de Fontete to retire, the first ball which struck the galley carried off the comite's head. The commander, now being near enough, cried out for M de Fontete to retire, which he did at once, and, by means of the sandbank, all escaped. During the remainder of that year's campaign, our commander had no desire to undertake new expeditions – his courage now quite cooled.

The following campaign, 1705, our six galleys were fitted out in the port of Dunkirk with M le Chevalier Langeron, my captain, now made squadron commander. His predecessor, having fallen so easily for the Dutch admiral's trick, having naturally retired after being raised to the dignity of a grand master of the Knights of Malta. M Langeron received one evening a despatch from the court, with orders to go as soon as possible with his six galleys to Ostend to strengthen the garrison, the town being threatened with a siege.

We immediately started, and having sailed all night, morning found us before Nieuport, nine miles from Ostend, where we could perceive along the coast a convoy of people and horse-drawn heavily-laden waggons escaping from Ostend. While we were still outside the sandbank, we sent the boat onshore, which was told that the army of the allies was within sight of Ostend, and that the town would be occupied that very day. Soon after, we saw a large naval armament advancing from the north, crowding all sail to cut us off from the channel of the sandbank between Ostend and Nieuport.

We were more than an hour in advance of this fleet, and could easily have entered Ostend before them, but our commander reflected upon the extreme peril to which we should be exposed in that port. The enemy fleet could very easily send fire-ships among us. Besides which, if the allies took the town, they would also take the galleys, vexing the King extremely. Everything considered, and a council of war having been held, it was resolved to return to Dunkirk, rowing as hard as we could.

Ostend was besieged by land and sea, and was obliged to surrender at the end of three days, not for want of a sufficient garrison, but because there was too large a one. For Count de La Motte, who was in the neighbourhood with a camp of twenty-two battalions and several squadrons of cavalry, threw himself with all his troops into the town, which was a great blunder, for the allies, only having attacked the place by firing bombs, red-hot shot, and shell, so many people, pressing one upon another in this little town, could neither move nor obtain shelter from these infernal machines, which rained down upon them; so they were obliged to surrender on condition that they might depart sword in hand, and not take arms again for a year. Our commander, the Chevalier de Langeron, for his part, was praised and rewarded by the court, because he had not executed its orders.

We passed all the summer in Dunkirk, only venturing out in calm weather, or with an east, north, or northeast wind, for if a west or southwest wind had caught us at sea, we should not have known where to run. As usual, we disarmed in the month of October for the winter, to await the next April when we would arm again to enter on the campaign.

5. We almost perish in a great storm, Dunkirk 1707

IN 1707, as there was a great deal of east wind, we cruised all over the Channel; taking one small English privateer, and burning another, until came the day when we all almost perished. Being in Dunkirk, in the finest weather possible, not a cloud on the sky, M de Langeron, impatient to cruise the English coast, called all the most experienced pilots to ask them if they saw any sign of the weather changing. For, because of their low freeboard, in bad weather the galleys cannot keep at sea. All the pilots agreed that the weather was settled, and would continue fine.

However, we had on board our galley, as a pilot, a poor fisherman of Dunkirk, named Peter Bart, brother of the celebrated Jean Bart, 'Admiral of the North'.[36] Peter, though much given to dissipation, drinking gin like water, knew the coasts well, and was also an expert observer of weather conditions, but because of his habits had no great credit with those who made the decisions. However, he had been invited to this council, where, in very bad French, he told our commander, 'Go to sea, and I promise you a good storm tomorrow morning.' All laughed at this, and, notwithstanding his entreaties, our galley, and that of M de Fontete, put to sea in such beautiful weather we might have held a lighted candle at the top of the mast. We cruised the shores of Dover, making our guns roar during the night; after which we returned to the French coast to Ambleteuse, a village situated between Calais and Boulogne where there was a sheltering cove between two cliffs, safe from the east and northeast winds, but full of rocks. I do not know what fancy took our commander, but he persisted in anchoring in this cove. M de Fontete, who was wiser, elected to remain in the open roadstead.

Directly Peter Bart saw we were to anchor in this cove, he began to shriek like a madman, saying at sunrise we should have as violent a storm as we had ever seen, and that the entrance of this cove being in the teeth of this wind, we should not be able to get out and would be dashed onto the rocks and the galley smashed to pieces – not even the ship's cat would be saved! They laughed at this, and we entered the cove just before dawn and put down two anchors. Everyone thought of getting a little sleep, except Peter, who wept, as he said, at the approach of inevitable death.

Day finally dawned, with a soft wind from the southwest, so soft no one took any notice of it. But as the sun rose, the wind increased, until the captain finally decided to leave the cove. But now a real tempest blew, so suddenly, that instead of weighing our two anchors we were obliged to cast out two others against the violence of the wind and waves, driving us back upon the rocks, now quite close to the stern of the galley. The worst of all was the anchorage ground in the cove was rocky and good for nothing. The four anchors were dragging, and could find no hold. M de Langeron, seeing this, commanded we row towards the anchors so as to relieve them, but immediately we dipped our oars into the sea, huge waves carried them out of our hands. Everyone then imagined shipwreck was inevitable, and all cried, groaned, and prayed.

The chaplain exposed the Holy Sacrament, and gave a blessing, offering general absolution to those slaves who felt real contrition. But they, instead, cried aloud to the chaplain, and the captain and his officers, 'Come, gentlemen, have courage! We shall all soon be drinking out of the same glass!' At last, though it galled him, the commander approached Peter Bart.

'If only I had believed you, Peter,' said he. 'Have you no expedient to save us?'

'By God's grace,' said Peter, 'I do. But what good is it if I am not listened to?' The commander immediately assured him that now his only wish was to listen to anything Peter might say.

'Well,' said Peter, 'first I declare that if my own life was not involved, I would leave you all to drown like the pigs you are!' Obviously, at such a time, this impertinence was readily pardoned.

'Second,' continued Peter, 'I will not be contradicted or opposed in any manoeuvre!' The commander at once gave orders, by beat of the drum, that Peter Bart was to be strictly obeyed, on pain of death. Peter asked the commander if he had a purse of gold.

'Of course!' said he. 'Here it is. Treat it as your own.' Peter took out four gold louis, and gave it back to him, then asked the sailors of the galley if there were four among them prepared to do what he asked, each to have a louis for drink-money. More than twenty immediately presented themselves, and Peter selected four of the most determined, whom he put into the large boat, called the caique, which is always on board the galleys when they go to sea. He made them take an anchor from the stern of the galley into this boat, though its cable was to remain in the galley to be told out as they rowed away from us. The boat was let down into the sea and Peter ordered them to cast the anchor upon the rocks upon which we were being driven. At this, everyone shrugged their shoulders, not being able to understand what this anchor could do from the stern of the galley, as it was from the bows they felt it ought to be held. The four sailors succeeded, though with great difficulty, in casting the anchor onto the rocks –where it held.

At this, Peter, seizing the commander's hand, exclaimed, 'We are saved, thank God!' Still no one understood his manoeuvre. Peter now lowered the yardarm, to which he fastened the large sail, which he reefed, tying it with such knots that when he pulled the rope, the knots would loosen, and the sail at once unfurl. The yard was then hoisted up, and he ordered four men with axes to be ready to cut the four anchor cables cast from the bows of the galley. He then hauled in and tightened the cable of the anchor which he had cast from the stern against the rock, and told a man with an axe to be ready to cut it at his command. This all being done, he ordered the four men at the bows to cut the cables of the four ahead anchors. As soon as the galley was released at the bows she began to turn, because she was held firmly by the anchor at the stern, and, given time, would have turned right round. When Peter saw she had turned sufficiently to take a quarter wind into her sail, he drew the sheet of the sail. In a twinkling the sail was unfurled, and took the wind. At the same moment the cable of the stern anchor was cut, and Peter himself holding the helm, made the galley fly out of this fatal cove like an arrow from a crossbow.

We now had to run for the nearest port to obtain shelter from the continuing storm, Dunkirk being the only one to leeward. The difficulty of reaching it did not disquiet us: we were only forty miles or so away, and the wind, though furious, was favourable. We could have made it in three hours, even under only one small sail. But our officers were in the greatest anxiety, lest the tempest should drive us past Dunkirk and onto the Dutch coast, something the convicts ardently wished –

and the officers exceedingly dreaded. Eventually we ran into the roadstead of Dunkirk. Our galley had left all her anchors in the cove of Ambleteuse, but M de Fontete, who had followed us, gave us two. These we cast in this roadstead, where we would need to remain for six hours, till the tide was high enough to enter the harbour. During these six hours we were constantly between life and death as waves, like mountains, continually covered us.

We were all more dead than alive, wet to the bones, having neither eaten nor drunk for two days, because we could have neither bread, wine, brandy, or anything from under the hatchway, lest the galley should fill with water and sink. Everyone was at prayer, both on the galley, and in the town. Here, the Holy Sacrament was exposed in all the churches, and public prayers offered for us, all they could do to help as no boat, small nor great, could leave the harbour to render us assistance.

And now another danger threatened. The harbour of Dunkirk is formed by two long, high jetties, extending a mile into the sea, the heads of which form the entrance to the port. Vessels must approach this entrance from the south, because of a bar of sand in front of it, which makes it necessary to keep quite close to the southern shore, and then, by careful steering, turn sharp round between the heads of the jetties – an extremely difficult manoeuvre in rough weather, especially for galleys of extreme length. Moreover, the

heads of these jetties were at that moment covered by
the sea, on account of the tempest, and we only saw the
entrance in intervals between waves. Besides which, we
knew that in entering by that narrow mouth between
the two pierheads, if the galley touched them, however
little, she would be dashed into a thousand pieces and
not a soul would be saved. What was to be done? We
must enter the harbour or perish.

Our pilots, having lost their presence of mind, went
to awaken Peter Bart, who was now quietly drunk,
sleeping on a bench, soaked as he was by waves
sweeping over him. He was asked if he knew any way
to enter the port without being lost.

'Yes,' said he, 'as I enter with my boat when I return
from fishing – at full sail.'

'What!' said the commander, 'A galley can't enter
port at full sail because of the difficulty of managing by
helm. You forget it is by oars that it is steered!'

'You cannot steer by oars in this sea,' said Peter.

'It is that which puzzles me,' said the commander.

Peter laughed at the panic he saw, and told the
commander, however, that he could not prevent the
galley from breaking her prow against the Quai de la
Poissonnerie, once the harbour was entered, because
entering under full sail with such a wind – he would not
be able to stop her.

'What matters that?' said M de Langeron, 'it is only
wood. The carpenter will repair the damage.'

Peter then veered the cables, arranged the sails, and, ordering perfect silence, kept close to the southern shore as far as the mouth of the harbour, steering so skilfully, that he turned sharp round into the entrance between the two jetties, immediately dropping his sails. The mayor had set two or three thousand sailors, and other seafaring people, to throw ropes from the jetties to help us, but the thickest of these broke like threads, the galley finally breaking its nose against the quay, as Peter had foretold. M de Fontete's galley observed, and made, the same manoeuvre, and also entered the port successfully. The commander immediately offered Peter double wages to remain in the galley.

'Not,' said Peter, 'if you gave me a thousand francs a month.' And off he went.

We scarcely left Dunkirk harbour again all the year, and we dismantled early for the winter.

6. Our galley destroyed, the crew massacred, Dunkirk 1708

IN APRIL 1708, we re-armed, and during the whole campaign merely cruised the English coast, alarming the enemy sufficiently to make him keep his troops on the alert, but as soon as any large coastguard ship appeared, escaping quickly back to the France. This lasted till 5 September, a day which I shall never forget, and on which I received the marks of the three great wounds I still bear.

It happened like this. At the beginning of the summer of 1708, Queen Anne of England sent a large number of men-of-war to sea to cruise the coasts, and also a guard-ship of seventy guns, this latter being commanded by a concealed Papist, a Captain Smith, with very hostile intentions towards England. This ship not belonging to any squadron, he was at liberty to execute his treason. He therefore sailed to Gothenburg, in Sweden, where he sold the vessel, and dismissed the crew. He then went in person to the court of France to offer his services to the King against England.

The King gave him a warm reception, and promised him the first vacant captainship, advising him in the meantime, to go to Dunkirk and serve as a volunteer in M de Langeron's galley, where he would be treated 'with honour and respect'. Captain Smith realised this 'advice' was really a command, and so came to Dunkirk where he was received very politely by the Chevalier de Langeron, and entertained at his expense, and took part in all the aforementioned expeditions we made to the English coast.

Smith, always having his head full of projects to injure the English, wished to make a few sorties ashore to distinguish himself by burning a few villages. But as there were coastguards along the English shore, and bodies of land troops that our sailors feared like fire, these ideas were constantly discounted. Smith then began sending schemes to the court, one being to burn and pillage the little town of Harwich. The King approved, and gave orders to M de Langeron to follow Captain Smith's commands, and for the Master of the Admiralty to provide him with everything he might require. The six galleys at Dunkirk were placed under his command, and M de Langeron, although submitting with repugnance to the orders of a foreigner, obeyed with apparent good grace.

The galleys were prepared for this expedition, acquiring both combustible materials, and a division of marines, and on the morning of that fateful 5 September 1708, we put to sea with the best weather possible. And as a soft breeze from the northeast favoured us well, with very little sail we arrived off Harwich about five o'clock in the evening, and without rowing at all. Smith, thinking that it was too early, and they might discover us from the shore, ordered us to retire farther out to sea to await the night, before making the descent.

We had not been lying-to more than a quarter of an hour, when the sentinel at the top of our mainmast called out, 'Ships!'

'From where?' he was asked.

'The north.'

'In what direction?'

'Towards the west.'

'How many sail?'

'Thirty-six,' said he.

'Of what sort?'

'Thirty-five merchant vessels, and a frigate of about thirty-six guns.' In truth, a merchant fleet sailing from the Texel to the Thames with a frigate as escort.

Our commander at once held a council of war at which it was decided that, instead of undertaking the Harwich expedition, we should try and make ourselves master of this fleet – far more in the King's interest than burning Harwich – for the opportunity of seizing so rich a booty did not present itself every day. An expedition to Harwich could be undertaken at any time.

Captain Smith protested, asserting that we must follow the orders of the King, and not turn aside to any other enterprise, and also that we should steer back to the south to allow this fleet to enter the Thames without perceiving us. But the council of war kept firm to their resolution, secretly glad that they had an opportunity of causing the failure of the Harwich expedition, on account of their jealousy in being obliged to obey Smith.

After this decision, each captain received the commander's orders to attack the fleet, and so we hoisted fresh sail and rowed with all our might to meet it. Our orders were that four galleys should engage, and try to take possession of, the merchant ships, which are generally without means of defence, while our galley, the head of the squadron, was to join with that of the Chevalier de Mauviliers in attacking and overcoming the escorting frigate. Following these directions, four galleys sailed to surround the merchant vessels, while we, with our consort, made straight for the frigate, the *Nightingale*.

Seeing our manoeuvre, the frigate's captain, Seth Jermy, one of the bravest and most skilful of the age, as he proved himself on this occasion, gave orders to the merchantmen to force on all sail to gain the mouth of the Thames, while he himself spread his sails, and turned at our two galleys. Our commander, even though the galley which was to serve as our consort was half a league behind ours, was not much disturbed by the approach of the frigate, thinking we were strong enough to master it, and being soon within range, we fired at her, she not replying with a single shot. At this, our commander joked that the captain of this frigate was evidently tired of being an Englishman, and was going to surrender to us without fighting. And we now advanced so rapidly we were soon within musket shot, and our musketeers beginning to play upon the frigate, when all of a sudden she veered round as if to flee from us. As the flight of an enemy generally increases courage, our crew began to cry out to the men on board the frigate that they were cowards. The English took no notice of this, but turned her back on us, and gave us her stern.

This presented a chance of boarding, for the manoeuvre of a galley to board a ship is to bring the bow of the galley against the stern of the ship (its weakest part). The whole strength of a galley is in her bows, and here she has the greater part of her artillery. She therefore endeavours to force her bows into the enemy's stern, firing her five guns, before her crew scramble on board.

Our commander at once ordered this attack, bidding the pilot to steer straight at the stern of the frigate, to force our bowsprit into her. All the soldiers and sailors appointed to jump on board, were standing ready with naked swords and axes, when the frigate suddenly put her helm down and we found her broadside upon us, against which we shaved so closely that our oars were broken to pieces. The Englishman, who had anticipated this, was now ready with his grappling-irons, and hooked us on to his broadside. He then gave us a taste of his artillery, and as all his guns were charged with grapeshot, and as everyone on our galley was as exposed as if upon an open bridge or raft, a frightful carnage ensued.

Our bench, on which were five convicts and Isouf, the Turk, happened to be just opposite to one of the guns of the frigate, which was so near that by raising myself a little I could have touched it with my hand. This unpleasant neighbour made us all tremble, my companions throwing themselves flat, hoping to escape its fire. Perceiving, however, from the manner in which it was pointed, that its discharge would bear directly upon our bench, and that anyone lying down must receive its fire upon their bodies, I thus determined to stand straight up on my bench. Chained as I was, what else could I do?

Attentive to all that was passing on board the frigate, I now saw the gunner, with his lighted match, begin to touch-off the guns at the bows of the frigate, working his way towards us. I could not take my eyes off this man, who kept gradually approaching, applying his match to each gun in succession, till he came to the one pointing upon our vessel. At this, standing quietly, I commended my soul to God, and then suddenly I found myself not on the bench, but in the centre of the galley, as far off as my chain could extend, and stretched across the body of the lieutenant, who was killed. I then became insensible.

What follows is from accounts I pieced together later. Prior to the engagement, the English captain had placed in the rigging a number of his men, with barrels full of hand-grenades, which they now rained down upon us. Such was their aim, that all our crew were disabled, not only from attacking, but even from making any defence. Those who were neither killed nor wounded began laying flat to pretend that they were, so great was the terror among the officers, as among the crew. The enemy perceiving this, then sent forty or fifty men on board our galley, sword in hand, who cut to pieces any of the crew upon whom they could lay their hands, only sparing the slaves who made no attempt at defence. After they had hacked about like butchers, they returned to their frigate, continuing to pelt us with their guns and grenades.

M de Langeron, seeing himself reduced to this condition, and that not a person on board except himself seeming able to stand, hoisted with his own hands the flag of distress, thus calling all the galleys of the squadron to our aid. Our consort was soon up with us, and the four other galleys, which had already attacked and forced the greater number of the merchantmen to strike their sails, seeing this signal, and the peril of their commander, quitted their prizes to come to our assistance, allowing the merchant fleet to escape.

All the galleys now rowed with such speed, that in less than a quarter of an hour the frigate was surrounded, and was soon in no condition to fire either cannon or musket-shot, though not a man of its crew appeared upon the deck. Twenty-five grenadiers out of each galley now received orders to board. They had not much trouble in mounting, as there was no one to dispute their way. But once on the deck they soon found someone to speak to, as the frigate's officers were entrenched under the quarterdeck, and began pouring a murderous fire on the grenadiers. But the worst of all was that this deck was composed of a grating of iron. Under this grating were the greater part of the crew, through the apertures of which they struck at the legs of the grenadiers with pikes and swords, and obliged them to soon jump back into their galleys. At this a further detachment was ordered to board, but they, too, came down much quicker than they had gone up.

Eventually the deck-grating was broken through with axes and other strong instruments, and the crew forced from between decks and made prisoner. But the officers were still entrenched under the quarterdeck, and poured forth their shot unceasingly until they, too, were overcome, but not without loss. All was left now was the captain, who had shut himself up in his cabin on the quarterdeck, firing different guns and pistols, and swearing that he would not surrender so long as a breath of life remained in him. The frigate's officers, now prisoners-of-war, gave a terrible report of their captain, who, they said would set fire to his frigate rather than surrender: all the more alarming as the cabin in which the captain had shut himself was also the entrance to the powder-magazine. He could, consequently, fire it in a twinkling. And, the frigate exploding, the six galleys, and three thousand men, would share her fate. We now expected to be blown up in the air with the frigate. In this extremity, it was resolved to invite the captain, with civility and politeness, to surrender, promising him the best treatment possible.

He replied by firing his guns. Then it was decided to capture him dead or alive, and a sergeant, with twelve grenadiers, was ordered with fixed bayonets to break through the door of the cabin and force him to surrender. The sergeant broke through the door, but the captain, who was waiting for him, at once blew out the sergeant's brains. The twelve accompanying grenadiers fled, and it was not possible for the officers to make any other soldier advance, they saying, in their defence, that only being able to enter the cabin one by one, the captain would kill them all one by one.

However, the captain, who had only been resisting so long in order to give his merchant fleet time to escape, saw by their lights that these ships were now safe; and no longer turned a deaf ear to the summons that he should surrender, but saying that he would only surrender his sword into the hands of the commander of the galleys, who must come on board the frigate to take it. While all these protocols were being debated, the captain, seeing he could now do no more to place the fleet in safety, gave up his sword and they brought him down into the galley to our commander, who was surprised to see a very little man, quite deformed, and hump-backed. Our commander then complimented him, telling him that it was simply 'fortunes of war', and that he might console himself for the loss of his ship by the kind treatment which he would be shown.

'I have no regret,' replied Jermy, 'for the loss of my frigate, since I have saved the fleet. I resolved from the moment I saw you to sacrifice my ship and my own person for the preservation of the property which I had undertaken to defend. You will still find,' added he, 'a small quantity of lead and powder, which I had neither time nor opportunity to give you, left in the frigate. And if you treat me as a man of honour, I, or some other of my nation, will some day perhaps have the opportunity of acting in the same way towards you.'

This quite pleased M de Langeron, who, returning him his sword, said very civilly, 'Take back this sword, sir, you deserve all too well to wear it, and are a prisoner to me only in name.'

Soon after this, however, our commander had occasion to repent that this action. For the English captain, being introduced into the great cabin, immediately recognised the traitor Smith, upon whose head the price of £1,000 sterling was set in England, and rushed upon him, sword in hand, to thrust him through. Our commander then seized him by the arm to the great regret of Jermy, who protested that he would rather have taken Smith than the six galleys, Captain Smith, greatly offended, replying that the English captain and himself ought not to be in the same galley, and begging the commander to place his prisoner on another vessel. But our commander replied that the frigate captain being his prisoner, it was Captain Smith must go to another galley, which was done.

Our prize, the *Nightingale* was at once manned and turned for home, but we had to go much out of our way, and rely on the darkness of the night, to evade four light-decked ships which came out to give chase. And it was during that first night I regained my senses. Raising myself from the lieutenant's body, I returned to my bench. Because of the darkness I saw neither blood nor carnage. And by reason of the darkness, and my disjointed mind, I first thought that my comrades were still lying down, for fear of the cannon. Nor did I know that I was wounded, feeling no pain.

I first said to my comrades, 'Get up, lads, the danger is over.' Receiving no answer, I addressed myself to Isouf, who had been a janissary, and who boasted that he was never afraid. I said, jokingly, 'What, Isouf, are you finally now afraid? Come, get up!' And took him by the arm to help him. But his arm separated from his body and remained in my hand. With terror I finally perceived that he, as well as the four others, were literally hewn in pieces, for the shot from the gun had fallen directly upon them.

I sat down upon the bench, and was not long in that attitude when I felt something cold and damp streaming down my naked body. I put up my hand and felt it was wet, but could not, in the darkness, distinguish if it was blood. But soon found that it was, streaming from a large wound which went quite through my left shoulder. Then I felt another on my left leg, below the knee, as deep as the one in my shoulder. And a third, nearly a foot long and four inches broad, in my stomach. Although I was losing an immense quantity of blood, I could gain no assistance, all around me being dead, not only on my bench, but also the two adjoining, so that of the eighteen men who were in those three benches, I alone had escaped. And all caused by one cannon shot! Though this will easily be understood when I mention that these cannon were charged to the muzzle: first with cartridge-powder, then a long tin box, its size varying to the calibre of the gun, which was filled with large musket-balls and old pieces of iron. When they fired these guns the box broke, and the balls (the grapeshot) spread in an incomprehensible manner, causing fearful damage.

I was now obliged to wait till the combat was fully over and order restored, for everything on board the galley was in a total state of disorder. It seems no one knew who was dead or alive; there were only the piercing cries of the wounded. The coursier, the gangway passing down the middle of the galley, about four feet broad, was apparently so encumbered with dead bodies that none could pass over it; while the rowers' benches were equally full of the bodies, not only of slaves, but of sailors, soldiers, and officers. So much so that the living and unhurt could scarcely move, either to throw the dead into the sea, or to help the wounded. Add to this the darkness, and that neither torches or lanterns could be lit for fear of attracting English ships of war, and the terrible state of chaos and confusion, which lasted far into the night, can hardly be imagined.

At last, when the combat was ended by the surrender of the frigate, the other five galleys drew alongside, and began working diligently, but silently, to put us into order, for lights were seen proceeding from the direction of the Thames, and several signal guns were heard. The first thing was to throw the dead into the sea, and carry the wounded into the hold. And God knows how many wretches were thrown into the sea as dead who were not really so, for in this darkness and confusion they took for dead those who had only fainted, either through pain, or from loss of blood from their wounds. I myself was in this extremity, for when the argousins came to my bench I had fallen into a fainting-fit, and lay unconscious among the others, bathed in their blood and my own. These argousins at once concluded all on our bench were dead: to be unchained and thrown overboard, a task so hastily performed that a bench was emptied in a moment.

After disposing of four of my comrades, they began unchaining me. Now it must be remembered that I was chained by the left leg, and that in this leg I was wounded. One argousin seized me by this leg, to drag me up, while another was unfastening the bolt of the iron ring which held my chain. The latter, happily for me, put his hand upon my wound, which caused me so much pain I raised a great cry, and heard the argousin say, 'This man is not dead!'

Imagining I was about to be thrown into the sea, I too cried, 'No! No! I am not dead!' They put me in the bottom of the hold among the other wounded, thrown on top of a cable. What a place for men agonised with pain! Sailors, soldiers, officers, and convicts, without any distinction, laid upon hard boards. No help or relief, for, with so many wounded, the surgeons could attend but a few. In three days in this terrible place, I had only a little camphored brandy applied to stop my bleeding – no bandage or further treatment; all around me the wounded dying like flies with the stifling heat, and overall the dreadful stench of gangrene.

At last we arrived in the roads of Dunkirk. There, we, the wounded, were hauled up out of the hold with ropes and pulleys, like cattle, and taken to the naval hospital. Here we slaves were separated from the freemen, and placed in two large wards containing forty beds each, each slave being neck-chained to the foot of the bed. At one o'clock in the afternoon the head surgeon of the hospital came to examine and dress our wounds, accompanied by all the surgeons of the ships and galleys which were in the harbour. And here, again, I was fortunate; for M Piecourt, having heard how our galley had lost so many men, had run at once to the harbour to inquire about me. Learning I was in hospital severely wounded, he had gone immediately to the head surgeon, a friend, and commended me to his care as warmly as if I had been his own son. And indeed, I can say that, after God, I owe my life to this surgeon, who undertook, contrary to his usual custom (for he never did anything but give orders), to dress my wounds himself.

At his first visit he took his tablets from his pocket, and asked who was called Jean Marteilhe. I replied that I was. He asked if I knew M Piecourt. I said that I did, and that it was M Piecourt, by his kindness, who had procured me all the indulgence I had received during my six years at the galleys.

'The manner,' said the surgeon, 'in which he has commended you to my care proves it. Now let me see your wounds.' The most dangerous was in the shoulder. The head surgeon took off the bandage which the galley surgeon had applied, he whose negligence had caused my wounds to gangrene. The head surgeon summoned this galley surgeon, and after reproaching him for being a butcher, commented that if I died, as he feared I should, the galley surgeon would be my murderer. The galley surgeon made the best excuse he could, and begged the head surgeon to be allowed to dress me. This was refused, the head surgeon declaring no one would dress me except himself.

As for the others, quite three-fourths died, the majority of whom were not wounded so dangerously as was I. This large number of deaths made some think that the English used poisoned balls, but I believe that this was a calumny deliberately spread because of the hatred the French bear the English. The opinion of the head surgeon was rather that the shot of the guns being dirty and rusty, added to the carelessness of the galley surgeons, was the cause of such mortality.

In less than two months I was healed, but the surgeon made me remain a month longer to regain my strength: while the hospital director, to whom I was also recommended by M Piecourt, ordered the brethren of the order of St Francis, who served this hospital, to give me all that I asked for which was not injurious to my health. And in truth, at the end of three months I was as sleek and fat as a monk. Upon discharge, the head surgeon wrote a certificate that, owing to my injuries, I was incapable of rowing or of doing other hard work in the galleys. After this, I was sent back to my usual bench.

7. At Dunkirk 1709

IN THE ENSUING CAMPAIGN, in 1709, we re-armed, as usual, in the month of April, though with my condition was very much altered. There are six convicts to each oar, the strongest and most vigorous always being strokesman, who has the hardest work. He is of the first class, the next is second class, and so on till the sixth class. This last is usually the weakest and feeblest slave on the bench. Before I was wounded I was of the first class, and the comite, whether by inadvertence or otherwise, had left me in this class, the work of which I could not perform, by reason of my shoulder wound, as at that time I was scarcely able to raise my hand to my mouth.

I placed myself then, of my own accord, in the sixth class, claiming to be maimed. This means passing through a test, which is this: the first time the galley puts to sea, to discover whether the convict is simply feigning from the hard work of the oar, the comite overwhelms the poor wretch with strokes of the lash till he is very nearly dead. We left the harbour for the first time that year, and after the comite (who always stands on the prow of the galley till she is out in the

open sea) had directed the starting of the galley, he
visited each bench to see how the rowers were classed.
He held a thick cord in his hand, with which he lashed
those who were not rowing according to his fancy. I
was in the sixth bench from the stern, and as he had
begun his inspection from the bow, and was much
excited, striking on all sides, I expected that he would
treat me pitilessly. He arrived at last at our bench, and
stopping with a ferocious air he ordered the strokes-
men to cease rowing.

Then, addressing me as, 'Dog of a Huguenot,' said
he, 'Come here.' I dragged my chain to approach the
coursier upon which he was standing, believing that he
had ordered me near that he might flog me better. As I
waited, cap in hand, in a supplicant posture, he said,
'Who ordered you to row?'

I replied that having only the use of one arm as he
could see by my scars (for I was, as usual, naked to the
waist), I was employing it as best I could to help my
comrades.

'That was not what I asked,' replied he, 'I asked you
who ordered you to row?'

'My duty,' replied I.

'Then I,' said he, 'command you not to row, nor any
other of my crew in a similar condition, for if those who
are wounded in battle cannot be released according to
the law, I will not have them to row in my galley.' Mark
that it is the law to release all those who are wounded

in a battle, however heinous the crime for which they have been condemned to the galleys, *except* the Protestant Reformed. And that the comite spoke as he did so that the other galley slaves would approve, and not think that he favoured a Protestant.

As I listened to these words as if an angel of heaven had appeared and uttered them, he called the argousin, saying, 'Unchain this incapable dog, and put him in the storeroom.' This is the place in the hold where all the victuals are kept. The argousin unchained me from that bench where, for seven years, I had suffered so much, and we descended to this store-cabin whilst the galley proceeded on her way, without the aid of my arms.

The galleys, that day and night, cruised the Channel, after which they returned to Dunkirk, where, as soon as we had anchored, the comite, seated on the table of his bench, called me to him.

'You have seen what I have done to relieve you,' said he, 'and how I have found this opportunity to esteem you, and all those of your religion, for you have done no harm to any one; and if you are damned on account of your religion, you will be punished enough in the other world.' I thanked him as well as I could for these sentiments and his kindness.

'But I am perplexed,' continued he, 'as to how I shall manage this affair and not to make an enemy of the chaplain, who will never suffer me to favour a Huguenot. However, I have thought of an expedient which will, perhaps, succeed. M de Langeron's secretary is dead, and he needs another. If I propose you, and in such a way he may accept you; you will then not only be exempt from work, but even respected; and I shall be protected from the censure of the chaplain. Go away,' said he, 'to the store-cabin; you will soon be called.'

The comite went immediately to M de Langeron, saying he had a man on the sixth bench, but would rather have a sheep here, for this dog was maimed of one arm. That he, the comite, had put him to the test by severe blows of the lash, but he really was incapable and thus prevented his comrades from rowing. M de Langeron asked him how I had been maimed.

'By wounds,' replied the comite, 'received at the capture of the *Nightingale*.'

'How comes it, then,' said the commander, 'he has not been released like the others?'

'Because,' said the comite, 'he is a Huguenot. But,' he added, 'this fellow knows how to write, and is well behaved, and I think if you want a secretary . . .'

'Call him,' said the commander. I was summoned, and directly the commander saw me, asked if I was not M Piecourt's friend. I told him that I was. 'Then you shall be my secretary,' said he. Then to the comite, 'Send him to the store-cabin, but remember no one is to give him orders but myself.'

Installed as the commander's secretary, and knowing he liked neatness, I had a little red coat made (a convict is obliged to wear that colour), received permission to let my hair grow, bought a scarlet cap, and, thus polished up, presented myself. The commander seemed charmed, and ordered his steward to give me at every meal a plate from his table, and a bottle of wine a day, which was done throughout the campaign of 1709. In truth, I wanted nothing except liberty, as I was night and day without the chain, having only an iron ring round my ankle. I had a good bed and rest, and while all the others were working at the oars, I was well fed, honoured and respected. I had, indeed, at certain times, very much to write, and sometimes passed whole nights thus that I might complete my work before it was expected. In this happy state I continued till the year 1712, when it pleased God to submit me to a trial, great in itself, and all the more bitter because nearly four years of ease had accustomed me to prosperity.

In the years 1710, 1711, and the greater part of 1712, the galleys had remained unarmed in the port of Dunkirk, France being so denuded of everything connected with her navy that she could not even arm a boat, so that no event worthy of notice occurred till 1 October 1712, when they removed us from the galleys at Dunkirk to those at Marseilles. But before I come to this removal, I must relate an event which placed me and others of our brethren in extreme peril of dying under the bastinado.

I have told how that good man, Isouf, was killed at

the battle in the Thames – he whose arm I took up in my hand, as I have already narrated. I was much grieved at his death, but now did not know who to serve me in my perilous relations with the banker, M Piecourt. But I had not the trouble of seeking, for ten or twelve Turks came to petition me, just as one petitions for a lucrative office. These good people, seeing that I did not know whom to trust, came one after the other, showing so much good feeling, and professing so much affection for those of our religion, whom they called their brethren in God, that I was moved to tears.

I accepted one named Aly, who served me for four years, till the time when we were removed from Dunkirk, and behaved with indescribable zeal and disinterestedness. Aly was so poor that several times I tried to make him accept one or two crowns, assuring him that they who sent us this money would desire he should have some share in it, but he always refused, saying, in his figurative style, that this money would burn his hands, and when I said once that if he did not take it I should employ another, he was like one in despair, beseeching me not to shut him out from the road to heaven. These people are called 'barbarians' by Christians, but in their conduct they often put to shame those who give them this name. And thanks to God's mercy, and the fidelity of Isouf and Aly, nothing unpleasant happened to me in the reception and distribution of the remittances with which I was charged during several years.

I generally knew pretty exactly the time when this remittance would be sent, and would despatch Aly (for the Turks are allowed to go anywhere without guards) to M Piecourt, who gave him the money for me, with a receipt which I had to sign, and which Aly then took back with any letters for our relations and brethren in Holland. But now M Piecourt had the misfortune to be embarrassed in his affairs, so that our remittance was entrusted to another Dunkirk banker, a M Penetrau. This gentleman two or three times paid me the money with punctuality and precaution, until he too became embarrassed in his affairs, and cast about for a plausible pretext for not paying me.

But before this I must speak of the chaplain who belonged to our galley and his reasonableness with us as regards our dealings with M Penetrau, which was because he was not of the usual sort who exercise this office in the galleys, which happened this way. The usual galley chaplains are secular priests of the society commonly called 'of the Mission,' or 'of St Lazarus' (which is why they are known on the galleys as 'Lazarists' or, more commonly, 'Missionaries'). This society was founded by Vincent de Paul, a simple priest, who by his pious reputation became the confessor of the mother of Louis XIV. De Paul was then charged to hold missions in the country for the instruction of the peasants and common people. This gave rise to the establishment of his society, which increased in time to establish branches in the most important towns in France, and to acquire many privileges, one being the nomination of military, naval, and galley chaplains.

These Lazarists insinuated themselves so well that, at court, the ministry regarded them as oracles, while the Jesuits could only seethe with envy and jealousy, for, notwithstanding all their cunning, the Jesuits had never foreseen the future greatness of the Lazarists, as these latter had well concealed their ambitions under a cloak of humility. They had seen how a seemingly humble exterior, and an air of mortification, had served the Jesuits, and they, therefore, imitated them in their dress and behaviour, and even surpassed them in the coarseness of their robes and in their negligent and almost dirty appearance. This so imposed upon the public and upon the court, that they obtained the care of the chapels and royal palaces, the administration of a number of seminaries, and the possession of the immense wealth they now enjoy. So powerful and formidable were these in my time at Marseilles, that if any of the King's officers displeased them they soon obtained a warrant to have them disgraced – and became so feared that all submitted to their tyranny. These fathers, then, having the spiritual direction of the galleys, placed in them men like themselves, cruel persecutors of all Huguenots.

But our chaplain having died in the English Channel,

M de Langeron, on account of the distance, which acquitted him from the necessity of waiting for the nomination of the Missionaries, but who would not be without a chaplain, took on board a monk of the Dominican order. A chaplain who at first treated us as badly as he could, but in time he conformed to our captain's way of behaving towards us, which succeeded into obliging acts towards us all, and especially me.

Since I had become M de Langeron's secretary, I had often the opportunity of conversing with this chaplain, and during the final three years I remained at Dunkirk scarcely a day passed that we did not talk an hour or two. He was a learned man, and as I often, by means of my friends, received religious books from Holland, he asked me one day if I had not some sermons of our authors to lend him. Though this request appeared suspicious, I nevertheless hazarded offering to him a volume of M Saurin's works, which he punctually returned to me. I then lent him all the books I had, even Jurieu's *Legitimate Prejudices against Popery*, which, as well as the others, he carefully returned. One day, in conversation, he asked me if we Huguenots did not receive money from Holland. At this point, I thought it best to reply negatively, for fear of the consequences which might ensue.

And now I return to the great danger I incurred regarding the distribution of the remittances. I have said that M Penetrau now conducted the business, but had become embarrassed in his affairs without any knowing of this. He now received an order from Amsterdam to pay me one hundred crowns, but being undone, cast about for a plausible pretext for not paying me. And although he knew he was about to sacrifice me, he went to our chaplain and told him that he had an order from Holland to pay me one hundred crowns, but as the grave warnings of the court made him afraid; he wished first to ask the chaplain's permission. His thinking being that the chaplain would immediately go to the master of the galleys; and that I should, after examination, be bastinadoed to make me confess the bankers who had previously paid me, he escaping by having laid the information against me.

The chaplain, understanding all this, looked fixedly at M Penetrau, and said, 'I am sure, sir, this is not the first time that you have made similar payments without asking my permission, and that your correspondents in Holland would hardly entrust you with doing so, without being certain you can well perform it. But, if you require my permission, I willingly grant it.' M Penetrau, much disconcerted by this, replied that as perhaps the chaplain's permission might not totally secure him from danger, he should approach the master of the galleys to ask him for his.

The chaplain, now annoyed, said sharply, 'What, sir! After you have given me to understand that my consent would decide you, you dare tell me that you will now apply to the galley master? Do so as you please! But remember those with whom you are dealing . . .' At this, Penetrau, fearful and vanquished, confessed that he was a little out at elbows, and though one hundred crowns would not bring him to extremities, he did not possess them at the moment, but that if I would agree to wait a fortnight, and not write to Holland, he would pay me without fail at the end of that time. The chaplain told him that he had done well to confess the matter to him, and that he would forgive Penetrau the threats he had used.

'But,' he continued, 'to ensure your punctuality, make me out a bill for the one hundred crowns, payable in fifteen days, which money I will remit to the person to whom you have to pay it. As to the Huguenot slave, I will pledge my word that he will not write to Amsterdam before the bill is due.' Penetrau, quite pleased that the matter had taken this turn, readily drew out the bill, and at the same time gave the chaplain the letter which he had for me.

That same day, the chaplain called me into the stern cabin and said at once with a serious air, 'I am surprised that a confessor of the truth dares to lie to a man of my character.' Quite aback, I told him that I did not know what he meant.

'Have you not told me,' said he, 'that you do not receive money from Holland, or any other place? Yet I hold in my hand that which convicts you of this falsehood,' and at the same time he showed me M Penetrau's bill.

'You know what this is?' said he.

'Yes, sir,' I said, examining it, 'Some money which belongs to you.'

'Not to me,' said the chaplain, 'but you.' And he related to me all that had passed, reproaching me for having lied. I took the liberty to tell him that he was no less guilty than I was, for knowing very well that it was not a thing which I could confess, he had obliged me to deny it by asking me. He agreed to this, and told me that in a fortnight he would bring me the one hundred crowns. This he did punctually, and in counting them out to me offered me his services.

'Write to your friends in Holland,' said he, 'They can address the remittances to me, which I will pay them punctually to you, by this means avoiding all risk.' I thanked him for his kindness, which, however, I did not think I ought to make use of, although this reserve on my part did not prevent our always remaining good friends.

Of the five Huguenots in the galley, the chaplain never molested one of us. On the contrary, he showed us a thousand kindnesses. These, becoming known to the Jesuits, they determined to punish him and addressed a memorial to the Bishop of Ypres, in which they accused our chaplain of being a heretic, and of loving and leaving Huguenots in peace, instead of forcing them to

enter the Roman Church. The bishop cited our chaplain
to appear before him to give an account of his conduct.
Our chaplain went to Ypres, where the bishop told him
that he had been accused of favouring the Huguenots in
his galley, leaving them in a quiet security without
trying to convert them.

'My Lord,' said the chaplain with firmness, 'if Your
Highness orders me to exhort them to conform to the
Roman Church, that is what I do every day, and no one
can prove the contrary, but if you enjoin me to imitate
the other chaplains, who cruelly persecute these poor
wretches, I shall tomorrow set out for my monastery.'
The bishop replied that he was content with his
conduct, and encouraged him to persevere in it; then
censured the other chaplains.

I have now reached the end of our residence at
Dunkirk, and the pains and suffering we had there, and
must now begin the description of the new fatigues and
tortures which were visited on us from 1 October 1712,
when they removed, or rather smuggled us off, from
Dunkirk to the galleys of Marseilles until our final
release, 17 January 1713.

8. We are removed with great torments from the galleys at Dunkirk to those at Marseilles 1712

EVERY ONE KNOWS that in the year 1712, the Queen of England made peace with France, and among other articles it was stipulated that the English should occupy the town and port of Dunkirk till they had demolished the fortifications and filled up the harbour. Consequently, the English came to Dunkirk in the month of September, with about five thousand men, waiting for the French garrison to evacuate and the galleys to put to sea. But as the French navy was reduced to such a deplorable condition that they could not even fit out the galleys, it was agreed that the galleys, with their crews and slaves, should remain in the harbour till they began to fill it up, which could not be done till after the winter, and that nothing should leave the harbour, neither boats, ships, sailors, nor galley slaves, without the requisite permissions.

The English no sooner arrived to take possession, than they ran in crowds to gaze on the galleys, vessels the majority had never seen before. Several English officers who were French Protestant refugees, and who had heard that Huguenots were confined in the galleys, immediately inquired for our number, and were told there were twenty-two of us. These officers immediately came to embrace us, pitying and weeping with us on our benches, indignant at our chains, and at our miseries. They remained a great part of the day, neither fearing the vermin nor the stench, taking pleasure in consoling us and exhorting us in the presence of the officers of the galleys, an example that attracted on board a large number of distinguished English officers, who also now testified to their piety by actions worthy of true Protestants. The soldiers, too, now crowded down to the galleys, and, in their zeal, swore that if we were not released willingly, they would do so by the sword.

The chaplains, fearing what might happen, begged M de Langeron to give orders that no one should be allowed to enter the galleys. This was tried, but the English soldiers only replied by placing their hands upon their swords, saying that, being masters of the town and the harbour, they were also masters of the galleys. So the galley officers were obliged to leave the plank free for any one who wished to come aboard.

An English colonel came one day to speak to me, and told me that the new governor of Dunkirk, Lord Hill, was probably ignorant of our detention, and of its cause, and advised me to draw up a petition to him for our release. I wrote this out as well as I could, and the colonel gave it to Lord Hill. The next day, His Lordship

sent his secretary to tell me that he would use every
effort to obtain our deliverance, and was about to write
to the Queen on the subject, and that her orders, sure to
be favourable, would determine his actions. He begged
us to wait patiently for another fortnight. This secretary
added that Lord Hill offered us his purse, had we need
of money.

I replied that we only needed His Lordship's protection, but I was very grateful for the answer to my
petition, and for the zeal he had shown. I then made his
reply known to our brethren in the galleys, and asked
them to avoid any conversation with the English
soldiers that might excite them to use violence to
procure us our liberty. After this, all was quiet as we
awaited the news from England. During the fortnight
which Lord Hill had told us to wait (it seems doubtful
whether he had really written to the Queen), he became
great friends with M de Langeron, and one day told him
that he could not understand how the French court
could have made the blunder of not making the
Protestant slaves leave Dunkirk before the English
entered. For surely the court could not be ignorant of
the horror with which the English nation regarded the
cruelties practised upon the Protestants on account of
their religion. And that the Queen would not fail to
deliver the Huguenots in the Dunkirk galleys, if only to
avoid a riot among the soldiers. M de Langeron agreed
with his friend that a great mistake had been made in

this matter, and begged for advice from Lord Hill, adding that the French King would never consent to the release of the slaves. Lord Hill mentioned an expedient by which trouble might be avoided.

'Write,' said he, 'to your court, requesting an order that the Huguenot slaves are to leave Dunkirk, secretly, by sea; I will provide a way for you, and the thing will be easy and without danger.'

M de Langeron did so, and soon received orders to act in concert with Lord Hill for our secret removal, which took place in the following manner. On 1 October, the feast of St Rémy, a fishing bark was chained to our galley, supposedly having been confiscated for smuggling by the English. That evening the rappel was beaten on the drum, as usual, and everyone went to bed. I was in my store-cabin, sleeping tranquilly, when I was suddenly awakened by our major, armed with a pistol, and accompanied by two soldiers of the galley, who placed bayonets at my throat. The major, whom I knew well, exhorted me in a friendly manner not to make any resistance, or he must execute the orders which he had to kill me.

'But what have I done, major?' asked I.

'You have done nothing,' said he, 'and no harm will be come to you if you are quiet.' He then made me descend quickly into the fishing bark, without either fire or light, and in great silence, for fear of being perceived by the English sentinel of the citadel. On entering the boat I found in it my twenty-one brethren, taken in the same manner as myself. We were chained down in the hold, on our backs like cattle about to be slain, each with a soldier of the galley holding a bayonet to our throats.

The boat was now unmoored, but to leave the harbour it was obliged to pass by an English ship, always stationed in the middle of the port to prevent anything from going out. This ship now summoned the fishing bark to her side, and inquired whither she was going. The master of the bark, an Englishman, replied he was going to fish for Lord Hill, and showed a note. The captain of the guard vessel took the note; it was written and signed in Lord Hill's own hand and read: 'Allow this boat, which is going to fish for my household, to leave the harbour.' The captain at once allowed the boat to depart. All those who commanded the forts in the harbour, and on the jetties, did the same, and at last we found ourselves in the open sea.

The soldiers now left the hold, shutting down the hatchways on us. We were now at liberty to arrange ourselves more comfortably upon the sand which served as ballast in the bottom of the boat. But as we knew that they never put to sea without provisions, if only bread and water, and as we had seen none on coming on board, we imagined that they were going to sink us, and that the soldiers would escape in the small boat attached to the bark.

The anguish into which this idea plunged us, and the terrible situation in which we found ourselves, being without light, can well be imagined. Some of us, seized with sudden fear, increased the alarm by crying out from time to time, 'Brothers, we are perishing, the water is coming into the bark!' At these exclamations each of us redoubled his prayers, thinking that it was the last moment of his life. It happened, however, that an old man of seventy did not believe it as firmly as the rest of us, and indeed he would have made us laugh had we been in less distressing circumstances. He was seated on his knapsack, and hearing them cry out that the water was entering, he stood holding his knapsack in one hand, eagerly feeling with the other to find a nail to hang it on. As he was near me, and his moving inter- rupted my devotions, I asked him what he was doing. 'I am trying to hang up my knapsack as high as I can,' said he, 'lest my clothes should get wet.'

'Rather think of your soul,' said I. 'If you are drowned, you will not want your clothes any more.'

'Alas!' said he, 'That is true,' and left off seeking for the nail.

At last it was day and they opened the hatchway, and as I was just under it, by standing up, I could see on to the deck. And the first person I saw was our master-at-arms, who I considered one of my friends, and on whose behalf, not long before, I had spoken a good word for him to our M de Langeron, our commander.

'What, you here, M Praire?' I said to him.

'Yes, my friend,' said he, with a smiling air. 'I don't think you slept too well last night.'

'But where are you taking us to?'

'Look,' said he, 'there is Calais,' pointing to the town, off which we now were. 'We are going to land you there,' he told us, adding we should not be making a long stay there, and should have to get our legs ready.

'But, sir,' said I, 'you are not able – neither are all the men in the world – to make men, decrepit through age, or maimed, or sick, as I am (I was then suffering from a fever) to walk.'

'In that case the King, who never asks what is impossible, will provide waggons for the infirm; and here, in the order of your route, there are directions to provide them for you. There,' said he, showing this order to me, 'see if there is not a waggon ordered for such like and for the baggage.' As I wished to see our destination, instead of looking at the beginning, I looked at the end of this order, and read: 'To Havre-de-Grace, where they shall be given over to the governor until fresh orders,' which information I passed on in a whisper, lest the master-at-arms should hear me.

They landed us at Calais where we were taken to the prison loaded with chains. The next morning the argousin, for one had accompanied us, fettered us two and two, each by a leg, and then passed a long chain through the rings of the chains which coupled us, so that the twenty-two of us, eleven couples, were all linked together. Now, it must be remembered, that amongst us there were old people, who, by age or infirmities, could not walk a quarter of a league, even if they had not been laden with chains. Several were sick, others worn out with misery and fatigue; and none of us had walked at all for a very long time. It was, therefore, impossible for us to perform four or five leagues a day, as our orders directed.

After they had chained us, I called our master-at-arms and said, 'Sir, it is impossible for us to walk in our present condition; I entreat you to provide one or two waggons to carry the infirm. You have a right to exact them wherever you pass.'

'I know my orders,' said he, 'and shall observe them.'

I was silent, and we started. We had not gone a quarter of a league when a small hill had to be ascended. This proved impossible for three or four of our old and sick who fell on the ground, and as we were all held by one chain, we could not advance, unless we had been strong enough to drag them on. The master-at-arms, and the soldiers of our escort which he commanded, exhorted us in kind words to take courage and to redouble our efforts, but against the impossible, nothing can be done. We all sat on the ground to give time to those who had fallen to rest, and as the master-at-arms was much embarrassed, and did not know what to do, I told him that in the circumstances there were two pieces of advice which I would give him, one of which he must take.

'Either shoot us, or, as I have already said, provide us with waggons. You will permit me to observe that, having never served except at sea, you cannot know what the King's orders are on an expedition by land. What they are, for a march, whether of soldiers, recruits, or criminals, is that if some are unable to walk, conveyances must be found, and taken in his, the King's, name. You, sir, must send a detachment of soldiers to the nearest village for as many waggons as you require to carry the infirm, while we will give you six francs a day for the hire of a waggon, which will be a clear profit to you, for in the King's service waggons can always be had free, and so these six francs will be yours.' Some of the soldiers confirmed what I said, which decided him to take my advice and two waggons were procured as far as the first resting-place for the night, and so from place to place as far as Havre-de-Grace.

The master-at-arms was a good sort of man, but not particularly clever. They had made him take an oath at Dunkirk not to reveal our destination. However, one day on the road, he rode up on horseback, to the waggon in which I was, and we engaged in conversation. While speaking on indifferent subjects, I asked our destination. Seeing that he evaded the question, I said it was useless his doing so, since I knew it as well as he. He defied me to tell him, which I did immediately, repeating to him what I had seen in the directions for our route, which he had shown me before we landed at Calais. The good man, not having remarked that I had looked at the last article in the document, was so astonished, he asked me, with great simplicity, whether I was a sorcerer or a prophet. I replied, that I was too honest to be a sorcerer, and too great a sinner to be a prophet.

'Besides,' said I, 'there is not one of us who does not know as much as I do, and you are making a great secret of a thing which is quite public among us.' We had, however, no reason ever to complain of him. He was very particular in giving us our rations at every lodging; but not being able to act beyond his orders, he could only lodge us in prisons, or in stables in those places where there were no prisons.

At last we reached Havre-de-Grace, where we had a better and more comfortable lodging than any we had had on the road. For it happened that though there were in the town a great many new converts to Romanism, they, notwithstanding their apostasy, were still zealous of the reformed religion. And these gentlemen, anticipating our arrival, and knowing that we were to be given into the charge of the governor, who was also the master of the marine, they went to beg him to show compassion. They reminded him that we poor chained prisoners had formerly been their brethren in faith, adding, that if he would have the kindness to treat us well, they would be greatly obliged to him, and would be responsible for us not endeavouring to escape. As these were Havre's richest merchants, the governor replied very graciously he would treat us as well as he possibly could.

'I have orders,' said he, 'to confine them in a place of security, but as these orders nowhere specify that it must be a prison, they shall have a comfortable lodging, with the same food as my own table; and you will have perfect liberty also to see them and assist them.' Matters being thus happily arranged, at Havre we alighted before the royal arsenal, where a large room awaited, belonging to the ropery, with mattresses, pillows, and counterpanes. On entering this room, we found the governor and our protectors, who embraced us with tears in their eyes, the governor appearing quite affected by this.

After which, the officials of the custom house arrived and asked the governor's permission to search us. He granted it, and they examined us at once, but without finding anything. But perceiving among our clothes a small locked box, in which we kept our books of devotion, they asked to examine that.

I at first refused the key, fearing the fire for our small library, but the governor said 'Give them the key, my friend, and fear nothing; these gentlemen must do their duty.' I gave it them with trembling; one of the officials opened the box, and seeing the books exclaimed, 'Here is Calvin's library; to the flames! To the flames!'

At this, the governor said, 'Rascal! Do your duty and nothing else, or I will teach you what to search for.' The official said no more, but shut up the box and went out. As soon as we were installed in our new abode, they took away the great chain which held us all together, leaving us only bound in couples. The governor then asked if we were content with our guards. We replied we had received during the journey as good treatment as they were able to give us.

'Then I shall leave them with you,' said he, and quartered them in a room opposite to ours. He also told the master-at-arms, that any of our protectors might come into the room to visit us between nine o'clock in the morning and eight o'clock in the evening, and that he should never interfere with any of our religious exercises. Henceforth our room was never free from persons of both sexes and all ages, and we had prayers morning and evening, read sermons, and sang psalms, so that our prison was like a little church. The tears of these good people being mingled with our songs as seeing our chains, and the resignation with which we bore them, they reproached themselves for their weakness, and lamented they, too, were not willing to resist unto death, instead of having grasped the allurements that had been employed to make them renounce the true religion, confirming that the Romish Church, instead of converting, only makes hypocrites.

The number of our weaker brethren coming to visit us now meant that all the churches of the town were emptied of their new converts, notwithstanding the prayers and menaces of the local Catholic priest, who complained to the governor, the latter replying he could not force people's consciences, that an open heretic was worth more than a concealed hypocrite, and that this occurrence had done much good, as now one could distinguish the good Catholics at Havre from the not-so-good.

With all this, no one was able to fathom the policy of the court in having us removed to Havre-de-Grace. Some thought that we were to be sent to America, and I have always believed that this was the original design of the ministry, for if their first resolution had been to send us to Paris to join the chain of the Marseilles galley slaves what was the use of sending us to Havre, nearly as far from the capital as Dunkirk? Probably, the scandal which we caused to the Roman Catholics at Havre caused the court to change its intentions concerning us, as we knew the priest had written to inform the court that our residence there had had an evil influence on his new converts, who had now deserted his church. So, once again, plans were set in motion to send us away as secretly as possible; although, just before our departure, a singular incident occurred which confirmed the master-at-arms in his idea that we were prophets.

On the fifteenth day of our residence at Havre, about nine in the evening, just as we and our guards were beginning supper, I felt a touch upon the shoulder. Turning, I recognised a young lady of good position, to whom I had lent a volume of sermons a few days before. She was wrapped in a shawl which she drew aside, saying to me in tears, 'Here, brother, I return your book. May God be with you in all your trials! For you are to be carried off at midnight; four waggons are ordered, and the white gate will remain open for your departure.'

I thanked her for coming at such an hour to give me this information herself, and asked her how she had been able to gain access to our room, which she had done with permission from the guard of the arsenal, whose house communicated with the ropery where we were confined. She added that, via Rouen, we were going to be taken to the frightful prison of the Tournelle, at Paris, to join the great chain which leaves every year for Marseilles. After wishing us constancy for this new trial, she departed as invisibly as she had entered.

For ourselves, we continued our supper very quietly, after which, instead of lying down to sleep, we began to pack our little luggage. While thus employed, our master-at-arms, according to his custom, came into our room for a chat for an hour while he smoked his pipe. Seeing us arranging our baggage, he asked us what we were doing.

'Getting ready to start at midnight, sir,' said I, 'and you should do the same.'

'You are mad,' said he.

'I tell you,' I replied, 'precisely at midnight there will be four waggons to take us out by the white gate, for you to conduct us to the prison of the Tournelle in Paris, to join the great chain for Marseilles.'

'And I tell you,' answered he, 'that I took the governor's orders at eight o'clock, and he told me that there was nothing new.' Just then, a servant came in, to tell the master-at-arms that the governor wished to speak to him. Shortly after, he came back, exclaiming.

'In God's name! You are a sorcerer or prophet! Although I think you are too honest to ask help of the devil.'

'I'm neither one nor the other, sir,' said I, 'and there is nothing but what is quite natural in that which surprises you so much.'

'But,' said the master-at-arms, 'I have heard from the governor's own lips, that no one in the town knows anything about your departure, except himself; so whatever you may say, I say God himself is with you.'

'I hope he is,' said I, and we continued to prepare for our departure. How the young lady became acquainted with this secret, we learned afterwards from her father, who visited us in the prison at Rouen, to give us a collection made for us at Havre. She was engaged to marry to the governor's secretary. The governor having received the letter from the court the evening before our departure, his secretary saw it and immediately told her, and she came to us.

At midnight the four waggons arrived, quietly, for the iron had been taken from the rims of the wheels, and the shoes from the horses' feet, so we might not be heard passing through the street. Each waggon was covered up as if to contain bales of merchandise, and with neither lanterns nor torches, we left the town. On arriving at Rouen we were conducted to the town hall to receive the magistrates' orders as to our lodging (as usual, the prison) but we were much surprised to be refused admittance by the gaoler who said he would rather give up his office than admit us. We went on to another prison, where the same thing happened, until finally they sent us to a tower which held the most infamous criminals. The gaoler here, receiving us under the strongest protest, cast us into a fearful dungeon, and, by the help of five or six turnkeys with swords in their hands, fastened our feet to huge beams of wood, so we could not move. Then, without giving us either light, bread, or anything else, he shut up the dungeon and went off. Hungry and thirsty, we called as loudly as we could for nearly two hours, that they bring us food for money.

At last some one came to the door, and we heard them say, 'Those people speak very good French.' This made us think that there was some misunderstanding and we continued to cry out, and to implore help for money – to be paid in advance! Upon this, the gaoler opened the door, and came in with his six turnkeys, and asked if we were Frenchmen. We said that we were.

'Then how is it you are not Christians?' said he, 'And worship the devil, who has made you more wicked than himself?' We replied that apparently he wished to joke with us, but would he please first find something for us to eat and drink. I gave him a louis d'or, adding if that was not enough, I would give him more.

'Truly,' he then said, 'you are not as you have been described. For during the last week they have spoken of you as devil-worshippers, and so wicked and violent, that they could not tame you in the Dunkirk galleys, and were sending you to Marseilles to bring you to reason.'

I recognised that this piece of malicious calumny came from the Jesuits, who had spread such a report that we might be regarded with horror and execration in Rouen, where there were many good Huguenots. I therefore told the gaoler our history, and the reasons for going from Dunkirk to Marseilles. Just then, our master-at-arms arrived in our dungeon to give us our rations. The gaoler took him aside, and asked him if we were as docile as we appeared.

'Certainly,' said the captain. 'I would undertake to conduct them alone through the whole of France; their only crime is that they are Huguenots.'

'Is that all?' said the gaoler, 'The most honest people in Rouen belong to that religion. I don't like it,' added he, 'but I like the people who belong to it: they are a brave set.' Addressing us, he then said, 'Tomorrow I shall tell your people, who will not fail to come and see you, and my doors will always be open to them.' He ordered his turnkeys to unfetter us, leaving only our usual chains, while he went to procure us refreshments.

Next day he kept his word, and brought several Huguenots to see us, who soon made the news of our arrival public, so that during the whole day our dungeon was never empty. They were so zealous and exhorted us in so pathetic a manner to perseverance, that we could not restrain our tears. Their ardour was so great, that several of them actually wished (after asking the permission of the master-at-arms) publicly to accompany us, on our departure, for about a league from the town, and help us by carrying our chains upon their shoulders. This we would never suffer, both on account of the humility which we professed, and to keep them from the trouble such an action would certainly have brought them.

We left Rouen in the same wagons, and I cannot sufficiently express the many acts of kindness which our master-at-arms showed during this journey; for besides the gratuities which he received from our friends at Rouen, he was firmly persuaded that we were saints favoured with the gift of prophecy. When the argousin was taking his usual precautions, as examining our chains, etc., the master-at-arms told him that he was taking useless trouble, for although we would go anywhere, voluntarily, if the King wished it; if we decided not to do so, neither all the argousin's precautions, nor those of all mankind, would be able to stop us.

On 17 November 1712, about three o'clock in the afternoon, we arrived at Paris. We alighted at the Chateau de la Tournelle, which was formerly a pleasure-house of our kings, but now served as a depot for all those condemned to the galleys for every sort of crime, and were conducted to the vast gloomy dungeon inhabited by those for the great Marseilles chain.

The dreadful spectacle which here presented itself to our eyes, made us shudder, and I confess that, accustomed as I was to dungeons, fetters, chains, and all other instruments of torture which tyranny or crime have invented, I had not strength to resist the fit of trembling which seized me, when I beheld this fearful place and all its horrors. It is a large dungeon, or rather a spacious cellar, furnished with huge beams of oak, placed at the distance of about three feet apart. These beams are about two feet and a half in thickness, and are so arranged, and fixed in some way to the floor, that at first sight one would take them for benches. But their use is much more uncomfortable. To these beams thick iron chains are attached, one and a half feet in length, and two feet apart, and at the ends of these chains is an iron collar. When the galley slaves arrive, they are made to lie half-down, so that their heads rest upon the beam; then this collar is put round their necks, closed, then riveted on using an anvil and heavy blows of a hammer. As these chains with collars are about two feet apart, and the beams forty feet long, twenty men are chained to them in file. This cellar, which is round, is so large, that they can chain up as many as five hundred men. There is nothing so dreadful as to behold the attitudes and postures of the wretches here chained. For a man so bound cannot lie down at full length, the beam upon which his head is fixed being too high; neither can he sit, nor stand upright, the beam being too low; I cannot better describe the posture of such a man than by saying he is half lying, half sitting, part of his body being upon the stones or flooring, the other part upon this beam.

It was in this manner that they chained us, and inured as we were to pains, fatigues, and sorrows, the three days and three nights which we were obliged to pass in this cruel situation, so racked our bodies and limbs, that we could not have survived it longer, especially our elderly, who cried out every moment that they were dying, and had no more strength to endure this terrible torture.

I may perhaps be asked, 'How can those poor wretches who are brought from the four corners of

France, and who sometimes are obliged to wait three, four, or even five and six months before the great chain starts, endure this torture?'

To this I reply, that an immense number succumb under the weight of their misery, and that those who escape death through strength of constitution, suffer pains of which it is impossible to give any adequate idea. For one hears in this horrible cavern groans and lamentations that would soften any other hearts but of the ferocious officials of this terrible place. The scanty relief of uttering these lamentations is even denied, for every night five or six brutes of turnkeys form a guard that falls without mercy upon those who speak, cry, or groan, barbarously striking them with huge ox bones.

With regard to food, that is tolerably good. The 'Grey Sisters' every day at twelve o'clock, bring soup, meat, and good bread in abundance. The duty of these sisters is to attend to the poor in Paris, to whom they take food every day, and even medicine if they require it. They also have the direction of several hospitals, especially those for soldiers, and by their rules are obliged to visit prisoners. In some places they instruct the young of both sexes. Whether they are capable of this, my readers may judge from what I am now about to relate.

The Mother Superior, who came every day to serve the galley slaves, always stayed a quarter of an hour with me, and gave me more to eat than I required. The other galley slaves often laughed at this, calling me the favourite of the mother abbess. One day, after giving me my portion, she said it was a pity we were not Christians.

'Who has told you that?' said I 'We are Christians, good mother, by God's mercy.'

'What!' said she, 'But you believe in Moses?'

'Do you not believe,' asked I, 'that Moses was a great prophet ?'

'I? Believe in that impostor?' said she, 'That false prophet who seduced so many Jews as Mohammed seduced the Turks! Oh, no! Thanks to the Lord I am not guilty of such a heresy.'

I shrugged my shoulders at this ridiculous speech, and contented myself with begging her to confess what she had just said to her confessor, who (if perchance he knew more than her) would certainly tell her what she said about Moses was a very great sin. One can judge from this whether these good women were capable of instructing the young.

I mentioned that for three days and three nights we were chained to the beams. The cause of our being delivered was as follows. A good Protestant of Paris, M Girardot de Chancourt, a rich merchant, having heard of our arrival, begged the governor to be allowed to see us, and to assist us in our necessities. The governor, though his great friend, said he could not allow him to enter the dungeon, for no one was permitted except ecclesiastics, but that M Girardot might look at us from the courtyard of the castle, through a double grating of iron, with which the windows of the dungeon were furnished. From here he could not speak to us, the distance being too great, but distinguished us by our red jackets, and was horrified by the frightful attitude in which we were placed, our heads nailed to the beams. He asked the governor if there was a means of chaining us by the leg, as were others of the galley slaves whom he saw much nearer the windows inside the dungeon. The governor told him that those whom he saw chained by the leg paid a certain price a month.

'Then,' said M Girardot, 'if you will, sir, give those poor fellows the same liberty, and I will pay you if they cannot.'

The next morning the governor came to the dungeon, and asked who had charge of our expenses. They pointed to me. The governor asked me if we should like to be at the grating, chained by the foot. I told him that we could ask for nothing better, and we agreed to pay him fifty crowns for the time that the chain remained at the Tournelle. I paid it at once from the common purse, and the governor had us unbound, and placed us as near as possible to the grating, chained by the foot. Having been accustomed to this for several years, we found ourselves quite relieved. The chain being two yards long, we could stand upright, sit, or lie down, and now found our situation a very tolerable one.

M Girardot often came to see us, and spoke to us

through the grating, but with prudence and circum-
spection, on account of the other, non-Huguenot galley
slaves who surrounded us, and at last brought us news
of our departure. We were to set out with the great chain
for Marseilles on 17 December. A week before this date,
the Jesuits, who have the spiritual direction of the
Tournelle, sent one of their novices, by his sermons a
great ignoramus, to preach to the other galley slaves to
confess and receive the Holy Sacrament always taking
the same text, 'Come unto me, all ye who are weary and
heavy laden, and I will give you rest.' Although shocked
by his absurdities, we never had the opportunity of
speaking to him, for he feared our conversation as he
would the fire, believing we were there to entrap good
Catholics, and in coming in and going out of the
dungeon, always made a great detour to avoid us.

Several Jesuit fathers, soon after, came to confess the
slaves, and bring them the Holy Sacrament. This they
made them take with their heads nailed down upon the
beams. A proceeding which appeared most irreverent,
even to us, and which filled us with horror. I noticed
that after they had given them the host, they made them
drink some wine out of a chalice, and asked one of these
fathers if the slaves received the communion in both
kinds. He replied they did not, that the wine given them
was not consecrated, but there only to make them
swallow the host. This was because of the story, which
the Jesuits pretended to believe, of a wicked galley slave

who made a compact with the devil that, if the devil would release them all, this particular slave would give the devil a consecrated wafer. to Satan agreed, whereby the slave kept the wafer in his mouth without swallowing after having received communion. The galley slave then giving it to Satan, the whole chain was set at liberty by the Evil One.

Shortly before we left, the superior of the Missionaries of Marseilles, Father Garcin, then visiting Paris, came to the Tournelle to exhort us, by worldly promises, to change our religion, always the point of their mission.

'I could obtain your release in twenty-four hours,' said he, 'if you would only recant. Think of what you are about to expose yourselves to. There is every probability that three-fourths of you will perish between here and Marseilles, at this inclement season, and when those who survive arrive at Marseilles, they will, as all the other Protestants have done, make their abjuration in my presence!' He then advised us he would see us at Marseilles to receive this abjuration.

On 17 December 1712, at nine o'clock in the morning, they brought us into the courtyard before the castle. They chained us by the neck, in couples, with a thick chain three feet long, in the middle of which was a round ring. They then placed us in file, couple behind couple, passing a long and thick chain through all the rings, so that we were thus chained together in a very long file – about four hundred slaves. Then we were made to sit on the ground to wait till the chief prosecutor of the parliament came to dispatch us, giving us into the charge of the captain of the chain whose name was Langlade, an officer under M d'Argenson, lieutenant of the Paris police. About noon the chief prosecutor, and three councillors arrived; called us by name, read out a copy of our sentence to each of us; and then gave them all into the hands of M Langlade. These formalities detained us three hours, during which M Girardot, who had not been idle in our cause, went to beseech M d'Argenson to recommend us to the captain of the chain. This he did very strongly, ordering M Langlade to distinguish us above all the others, to procure us all the relief in his power, and to bring back to him, after his return from Marseilles, a certificate, in which we attested that we were contented with him. He also directed him to arrange with M Girardot for our comfort during the journey. The chief prosecutor having kindly granted permission to M Girardot to come into the courtyard, he did so, and embraced us all with an affection worthy of the principles of that Christianity which influenced him. Then he talked to the captain, who told him that it was necessary that the money we had should be given over to him, because at the first lodging at which the chain stopped, we should be searched, and that galley slaves forfeit all money found on them.

M Girardot asked if we would trust our money to

the captain. We replied we would, and as I kept the common purse, I put it into M Girardot's hands, who counted it out to the captain – about eight hundred francs. The captain told M Girardot that, as we had sick and infirm among us, it would be necessary to provide one or two waggons. He added he could not do this at the government's expense, without severely lashing those who could not walk, to be certain that they were not malingering. M Girardot understood, and agreed that we should pay the captain one hundred crowns, so that, when we complained of not being able to walk, they might put us into waggons without striking us: one hundred crowns from the common purse to buy us off from blows during the journey. For our added security, M Girardot made the captain sign a receipt, with the promise that, in giving us back our money and our box of books (the carriage of which to Marseilles was included in our one hundred crowns), he would render up an account of what had been spent, and receive our attestation that we were satisfied.

This done, we left the Tournelle about three o'clock in the afternoon, and traversed a great part of Paris, that we might sleep that night at Charenton. A great number of Huguenots stood in the streets through which the chain passed, and, notwithstanding the blows which our brutal archers gave them, threw themselves upon us to embrace us, distinguished as were by our red jackets, and that we twenty-two were all together at the end of the chain.

Four gentlemen, rich Huguenot merchants of Paris, one of whom was a great friend of the captain, received permission to accompany us as far as Charenton, and made the captain promise to let them entertain us to supper, detaching us from the great chain, that we might be with them in a private room of the inn at Charenton, where the chain was to lodge. We arrived there about six in the evening, by moonlight. Although it had frozen terribly hard, the walk, and the excessive weight of our chains (150lbs for each, as our captain himself said), had so warmed us that, on arriving, we were as wet with perspiration as if we had been plunged into water. Here we were lodged in the stable of the inn; but, alas! What a lodging! And what a rest they prepared for us! We were chained so that we could only with difficulty sit, and then on a dung-heap. For the captain conducts the chain at his own expense as far as Marseilles, receiving there twenty crowns a head for each man. So he spares even straw, of which we had none during the whole journey. Here, for the moment, they left us to rest.

In the meantime, our four gentlemen from Paris had engaged the largest apartment in the inn, and ordered a supper for thirty persons, reckoning that the captain would keep his word to them. But how different an entertainment from that which they expected was the one in which we had to participate, and they to behold!

At nine o'clock, in bright moonlight, and with a very hard frost and north wind, they unfastened our chains, and turned us out of the stable into the inn's spacious courtyard, enclosed by a wall. They arranged the chain on one side of this courtyard; then ordered us, under blows from huge whips, to strip off all our clothes and to put them at our feet, we twenty-two, as well as the whole chain, being expected to submit. After we were naked, we were ordered to march to the other end of the court, where we were exposed to the north wind for two hours, during which time the archers examined our clothes, under the pretext of looking for knives, files, and other tools, but really all was a pretence for these harpies to take anything they fancied: money, handkerchiefs, linen (if at all good), snuff-boxes, scissors, etc. They kept everything, and any poor wretch asking for what had been taken from him, was overwhelmed with cuffs and blows.

This examination and robbery being made, the chain was ordered to march back to their clothes. But by now the greater part of these unfortunates, ourselves included, were so stiffened by cold, that it was impossible to walk even that short distance. Then the blows from the cudgels and the whips rained down on all sides, and this horrible treatment not succeeding in reviving some poor frozen bodies, they were heaped one upon another, some dead, others dying, the barbarous archers dragging them like carrion, by the chains round their necks, their bodies streaming with blood. Eighteen died.

We twenty-two were neither beaten nor dragged, thanks to God and our hundred crowns, which we considered to have been well employed. As the archers helped us to walk, and even carried some of us in their arms to the place where we had left our clothes, and, by a sort of miracle, not one of us perished there, or later. For, three times more on our subsequent journey this barbarous examination took place in the open air, with a cold as great and even more intense than it was at Charenton.

Whilst we were receiving this treatment, the four gentlemen from Paris saw from the window of their room what was taking place and entreated the captain with clasped hands to spare us, but he did not heed them, and all that these good gentlemen could do was to call out to commend ourselves to God, as people do to victims about to undergo the punishment of death. Nor would the captain allow them to go into the stable to assist us, nor to bring us the least refreshment. We were chained down again as before, with a piece of bread, an ounce of cheese, and a very small quantity of bad wine. We never saw those gentlemen again, and they could not have had much appetite for the supper which they had prepared for us.

Next morning we started from Charenton. Some of our twenty-two, who required it, being placed in the waggons without being in the least ill-used, but others, overcome with the sufferings of the preceding evening, some at the brink of death, could only obtain this favour by passing under the ordeal of the whips. After which they were detached from the great chain, dragged by their necks like dead cattle, and thrown upon the waggon like dogs. Their naked legs were left hanging out, and froze in a short time, causing indescribable torture. Any who complained were frequently killed by repeated blows of the stick.

It may be asked why the captain did not take more care to spare their lives, as he was to receive twenty crowns a head for those whom he delivered alive at Marseilles, and nothing for those who died on the road. The reason is that the captain had to provide conveyances at his own expense, and waggons being dear, he would not pay to hire them. To take a man in a waggon as far as Marseilles, would have cost more than forty crowns, plus the man's board. So it was more profitable to kill. Men who died would be left to the priest of the first village he passed, from whom he would demand an attestation of their burial.

Thus we traversed Burgundy and Mâconnais, as far as Lyons, nine to twelve miles a day: a great deal, considering our chains; sleeping every night upon stable dunghills, badly fed, and, when it thawed, up to our knees in mud, and afflicted with vermin and the itch. As to this latter, not one of us twenty-two caught it, though several of us were coupled with those suffering from the disease. The Huguenot I was chained to having hurt his foot, he was put in a waggon, and I was chained at Dijon to a man condemned for desertion, a good sort of fellow. He was suffering frightfully from this loathsome disorder, but notwithstanding its infectious nature, I did not catch it.

On arriving at Lyons, the chain was placed in large flat-bottomed boats, to descend the Rhone as far as Pont St Esprit, from thence by land to Avignon, and from Avignon to Marseilles, where we arrived on 17 January 1713, all twenty-two of us, thanks to God, in good health. Of the others, many died on the road; very few were not sick; many of whom then died in the hospital at Marseilles.

Once there, the main chain was soon divided among the thirty-five galleys then at Marseilles, but we twenty-two Huguenots were placed in a galley named the *Grande Réale*, which served as a depot for newcomers, and also as an infirmary for the others. We were not divided because they expected six galleys from Dunkirk would come to Marseilles, when we would rejoin those we had left. With those of our brethren already on board the *Grande Réale*, we were now more than forty Huguenots.

Father Garcin, as he promised in the dungeon of the Tournelle at Paris, came to us the day after our arrival, and counting the same number he had seen at Paris, said, 'It is wonderful that you have all escaped! But are you not weary of suffering?'

'You deceive yourself, sir,' said I, 'if you think that sufferings weaken our faith. On the contrary, the more we suffer, the more we remember God.'

'Nonsense!' said he.

'Not so much nonsense,' I replied, 'as that which you told us at Paris, that all our brethren in the galleys at Marseilles would abjure in your presence. We find not one here has done so, and I, were I in your place, should be ashamed at being discovered in such a gross imposture.'

'You are a reasoner,' he replied rudely, and departed.

Two or three months passed at Marseilles without anything particular happening, but about the beginning of April, the Missionaries made a general exhortation to us all, to persuade us to change our religion as they had heard, that in England, Queen Anne was being strongly solicited to put pressure on the King of France for our release. And, as good politicians, they were certain that if this Queen demanded it, the King, for reasons known to everyone, would not refuse it. So these gentlemen made the King, who was always ready to listen to them, believe that we 'heretics' at the galleys were about to come over to the Roman Church, that the King might thus have something with which to oppose any request Anne might make for our release.

But not having been able to persuade any of us to recant, and requiring someone to do so, what did the deceivers do? They persuaded two wretched convicts, one a thief, the other a deserter, both Roman Catholics, to pretend that they belonged to the Huguenots, and then to turn Roman Catholics. After which, they promised them their release. These two poor wretches lent a willing ear, and readily acquiesced in the proposal.

We, in perfect ignorance of this proceeding, were therefore much surprised one Sunday, when Mass was being said on the *Grande Réale*, to see one of these two pretend Huguenots roll himself up in his cloak and lie down upon their benches, as the real Huguenots do, this being allowed to those who professed to have no faith in the Mass. The reason for this toleration, which may surprise my readers, was as follows.

After the Peace of Ryswick, the Missionaries, when Mass was said in the galleys, wished the Huguenots to fall on their knees, bareheaded, the posture observed by the Roman Catholics. To effect this, they had not much difficulty gaining the support of M de Bonbelle, major general of the galleys, one of the fiercest of all persecutors. They arranged with him that the bastinado should be given to all Huguenots, till they observed the required posture. And to make this punishment the more fearful, the major should begin at one end of the galleys (there were forty) and give the bastinado to one or two galleys a day until he reached the end, and then begin again with those who remained obstinate, until they submitted or died under the lash.

Bonbelle carried out this abominable scheme; his favourite words in exhorting these poor martyrs to obey being, 'Dog! Down on your knees when Mass is being said, and if you won't pray to God, pray to the devil! What does it matter to us?'

All those who were exposed to this punishment endured it in a holy and courageous manner. Some kind souls, however, informed the ambassadors of the Protestant powers at the French court, who, at such an atrocious injustice, memorialised the King, saying it was disgraceful that men who were already suffering extreme hardships for refusing to conform to the Romish church should be assailed by new tortures to make them submit to it. The King confessed it was unjust, and said that the violence had been committed without his orders. He immediately sent to Marseilles to cease these excesses, and that reparation should be made to the Huguenots on the galleys. This was done by saying that it was a misunderstanding which should not occur again. But ever since Huguenots have been allowed to sit or lie on their benches during Mass, as mentioned above.

I must now return to the two false Huguenots, tools of the Missionaries. These wretches having lain down on their benches during Mass, the comite, part of the plot, asked the reason. They replied by swearing that they were Huguenots, because their parents had been so. The comite told the chaplains, for this scene took place on two different galleys. The chaplains exhorted them to return to the Church. They pretended to resist at first, but finally yielded. These two false Huguenots having made their public and solemn abjuration, received, a few days after, their pardon from the court, and were at once set at liberty. We fancied from the beginning that this was a trick of the Missionaries, but did not penetrate the real object of it, until the day of their release, when Father Garcin and another missionary went from galley to galley to announce this favour that they said the King had granted our two brethren.

They came at last to us forty on the *Grande Réale*, and ordered the argousin to unchain us all, that we might speak to them in the stern cabin. We went thither, and after the most flattering civilities, which the Jesuits always have to hand, they began their harangue thus.

'Gentlemen, you know the pains and the cares which we have always taken for your conversion, but have been disappointed, however, in not reaping all the fruits we hoped. But as God disposes, two of you, to whom the Saviour gave grace to listen to us, embraced our truths, and with great zeal made their abjuration. And as nothing gives His Majesty greater pleasure than the conversion of his erring subjects, we informed him of this, and this is what he has ordered his minister, M de Pontchartrain,[37] to write to us.' Then they read the minister's letter, the substance of which was that His Majesty had been glad to learn that two of the principal Calvinist heretics in the galleys had renounced their errors, and His Majesty hoped, from information that had been given him, that soon all the others on the galleys would follow their example, in which case His Majesty promised not only release, but also his royal favour.

We judged from this letter that the Missionaries had played this trick in order to make His Majesty believe that these two conversions were the buttresses which would sustain many others; and that, having this idea, His Majesty would not listen to any solicitation from England in our favour, supposing we were all on the point of conversion.

After Father Garcin had read M Pontchartrain's letter to us, and exalted the King's fatherly kindness, he then dilated on the goodness and gentleness of the Romish church, which, following the example of the Saviour, only drew men by persuasion.

'Do not allege,' exclaimed this father, 'that we persecute you – far from us is that system of persecution you so often raise. We detest and abhor it, and agree with you it is not right for any to persecute others for their religion. Simply reflect for a time,' he continued, 'then yield yourselves to the pious solicitation of His Majesty, and to the gentle persuasion of our truths, put forward with a real zeal for your salvation.'

Having heard this, one of our number then spoke. He testified we were very sensible of the offers, so full of kindness, which His Majesty had made, and that we should continue all our lives to be good and faithful subjects of His Majesty. But as to our faith, we were resolved to profess it with heart and lips, even to our lives' end. Here Father Garcin interrupted, saying one man could not answer for us all, and that each of us should reflect in private upon what we had just heard. At this we left the cabin, where they remained a little longer, apparently to see if some few among us might not return to declare themselves convinced.

As the argousin began to chain us each to our several benches, I conversed with three of our brethren and told them that I was anxious to answer Father Garcin's daring to assert we were not persecuted. These replied that, knowing as we did the harsh and cruel character of these fathers, we could only expect that any argument with them, however humble, would only result in further ill-usage.

'Gentlemen,' said I, 'we have suffered so much, that anything more will not astonish us. I beg, therefore, that we four return to these fathers, that in your presence I may state what I feel in my heart. But I promise that no invective on my part shall furnish them with a pretext for ill-treating us.'

They consented, and we re-entered the cabin. Directly they saw us coming in, the fathers put on a cheerful air, persuaded that we had come to confess ourselves vanquished. Saluting us in the most amiable manner, they offered us seats. Father Garcin then asked if we had reflected upon what he had said, and on the King's promise. I replied we were fully persuaded of the sincerity of His Majesty, but that we still had several queries. I must confess that my manner was rather hypocritical, but I wished to make them tacitly confess that we were persecuted for the sake of our faith; especially there was one great obstacle to what they called our conversion, which we were now going to ask him to remove.

'Then speak, sir!' cried Father Garcin, joyfully, 'And be satisfied!'

Thereupon I said, 'I certify that thanks to God and my parents, I have been brought up in the reformed religion, but must confess that nothing strengthens me more in it than to see myself persecuted for its sake. For when I consider that Jesus Christ and so many faithful Christians have been persecuted, I cannot but believe myself to be in the right road to salvation, since I am persecuted also. Thus, sir, if you can prove to me that we are not persecuted, as you asserted just now, you will gain considerable advantage over me.'

'I am delighted,' replied Father Garcin, 'that you have clearly made known your scruples, and equally delighted that there is nothing so easy as to prove to you that you are not persecuted for your religion. Do you know,' he then asked me, 'what persecution is?'

'Alas, sir!' said I, 'Our condition has made us only too well acquainted with it.'

'Pshaw!' said he, 'There is the mistake you make: taking chastisement for persecution. Why are you at the galleys? What is the motive of your sentence?' I replied that, finding myself persecuted in my own country, I had wished to leave the kingdom to profess my religion in liberty; but had been arrested and condemned to the galleys.

'Do you not see,' exclaimed Father Garcin, 'that you do not know what persecution is? Persecution consists in being badly treated to oblige you to renounce the religion which you profess. But in your case, religion has nothing to do with it. The King has simply forbidden his subjects to leave the kingdom without his permission. You attempted to do this, and were therefore chastised for having disobeyed the King's orders: a police matter; but not one of church, or religion.' He then addressed another of our brethren present, to ask him why he was at the galleys.

'For having prayed to God at a religious meeting,' replied this brother.

'More disobedience of the King's orders,' said Father Garcin, 'who has forbidden his subjects to meet in any place to pray to God except in parish, and other, churches of the kingdom. Again, you are being punished only for having disobeyed the King's orders.'

Another then related how, when he was very ill, the local priest had come to his bedside to ascertain whether he would live and die a Huguenot or a Roman Catholic.

He had replied a Huguenot, and, on recovery, was arrested and condemned to the galleys.

'Another act of disobedience,' said Father Garcin. 'The King wishes his subjects to live and die in the Roman religion. On refusing to do so, you, too, disobeyed orders. Gentlemen, it is all about obeying the King's commands; the church has no part in it. All that has happened, has happened independently of her knowledge.'

I now said with a simple air that I was content with his explanation as to what persecution was, but wanted to know whether, if my other doubts could be cleared up, I might be released before making my abjuration.

'Certainly not,' replied Father Garcin, 'you will never leave the galleys till you have made it in its complete form.'

'And if I make this abjuration? I can then be released soon?'

'A fortnight,' said Father Garcin, 'for the King promises it to you.'

I then resumed my natural air, saying, 'You have endeavoured, sir,' said I, 'by sophistical reasons, to prove we are not persecuted on account of our religion; but I, without any philosophy or rhetoric, in my last two simple questions, have made you confess that it is our religion which keeps us in the galleys; for you assert that if we make formal abjuration, we would be set free at once. But on the contrary, that there will never be any liberty if we do not abjure!' At this, this father saw himself so thoroughly entrapped by his own mouth, and, fury overpowering his senses, he cried to the argousin to come and chain us to our benches without the slightest alleviation. This incident shows the diabolical character of these Missionaries.

I now pass on to the events which gained us our liberty, but before doing so wish to show persecution as only the Missionaries can inflict it. I have spoken of the great risks run by those who receive the charitable monies sent to us from abroad, the one who distributed them at Marseilles being M Sabatier. Unlike Dunkirk, at Marseilles the Missionaries, not content with watching till they could catch someone in the act of paying money to the Huguenots in the galleys, often conducted searches where, on the firing of a gun, the sous-comites, and petty officers of the galleys threw themselves upon the poor Huguenots, searching them most severely while lashing them, and confiscating on the spot all monies, books of devotion, and letters. These examinations were performed with great strictness, and the Missionaries, fancying the Huguenots gave their property to the Romish convicts, or to the Turks on their bench, to hide, took to keeping the day and hour of this search quite secret, and by this means took Sabatier.

Sabatier, in charge of receiving and distributing the remittances at Marseilles, did so by the help of his faithful Turk, but also had to distribute the money to the other brethren in their separate galleys. To do this he would fold the portion of money which was to go to each galley, which his Turk would then convey to a Huguenot brother in those galleys. As the Turk was necessarily obliged to go often to Sabatier's bench to receive these commissions, the comite began to suspect something, and informed the major of the galleys. The major gave orders that the Turk should be watched when he came from Sabatier, and that if he then left the galley he should be seized and examined. This did not fail to take place and the Turk was seized, and the money was found on him, together with the list of those among whom it was to be divided. The Turk was asked from whom he had received this money. He would not tell, but it had been seen that it had come from Sabatier, who now openly confessed that he had given the packet to the Turk. The major was delighted, hoping now they would at last discover the Marseilles banker and reported his success to the Marseilles galley master.

This man had the gout and could not go to Sabatier's galley that he might make him confess by the torture of the bastinado, so he ordered Sabatier to be chained to a Turk, and brought by a guard into his presence. At his house, the galley master at first spoke amiably enough to Sabatier, telling him that as he made so great a profession of telling the truth, he hoped he would do so now. Sabatier replied that he would speak the truth about everything which concerned himself, even at the peril of his own life.

'Well,' said the Marseilles master, 'confess the truth, and you will not be harmed.' And then asked if the packet and money and the writing in which it was wrapped up came from him.

'Yes, sir,' replied Sabatier. When asked to whom he was sending the packet, Sabatier replied that he was sending it to one of his brethren in the faith to distribute the money to the others who were on the list.

'For what purpose is this money?' inquired the master. Sabatier replied that it was sent out of charity to ease them in their slavery.

'From whence does it come?'

'From Geneva, sir,' replied Sabatier.

'How often?'

'From time to time; when our friends think that we are in want of it.'

'In what manner do you receive it?'

'Through a banker of Geneva, who remits it to a banker at Marseilles.'

'And the banker's name?' asked the master.

'Sir,' said Sabatier firmly, 'so far I have been able to tell, as I promised, the real truth as it concerns myself. And if you find what I have said and done criminal, punish me as you think proper. But I will not denounce a man who has only acted out of kindness to us, and whose ruin I know my deposition would cause.'

'Wretch,' said the master, 'How dare you refuse? You will either tell me or expire under the lash!'

'No.' said Sabatier. The master, transported with rage, ordered the guard who had brought Sabatier, to beat him with a stick. But this guard, deeply touched, and who had known Sabatier well for several years, replied, 'Sir, he is a brave man; I cannot strike him.'

'Rascal!' said the master, 'Give me your stick.'

The guard having done this, the master made Sabatier approach his chair, and then broke the stick upon his body, Sabatier not making the least complaint, nor changing his position to avoid the blows. Not able to beat him any longer, as his strength failed him, the master ordered Sabatier to be led back to the galley, and commanded the major of the galleys to bastinado Sabatier until he died, or confessed the name of the banker. The punishment took place immediately without any form of trial. Sabatier endured with constancy this extreme barbarous treatment, and as long as the power of speech remained to him continued to call upon God, praying him to grant him grace to resist even unto death. And when speech and motion failed, they still continued to strike to the utmost his poor mangled body.

The surgeon of the galleys, watching if he still breathed, said to the major that if they struck him now, ever so little, he would certainly die, and his secret with him. But if they revived him, they might begin again. To this the major assented. They rubbed his mangled back with strong vinegar and salt. The pain which this application caused made him revive, but he was so weak they saw they would kill him at the first blow. They thought it best therefore to take him to the hospital, that he might regain sufficient strength to undergo a second punishment. But he was so long hovering between life and death, that either the lapse of time made them forget him, or that even his executioners dreaded exercising such a punishment for a cause which did them no honour, and he was not again exposed to this torture. He recovered, but was always so sickly and weak in the head, that during the few years he lived afterwards, he could not carry on the simplest conversation. And his voice was so low that he could scarcely be heard. Such are the Missionaries of Marseilles!

9. The last of the chains 1713

THE PEACE OF UTRECHT being concluded without anything having been done for us, the Marquis de Rochegude, a French refugee in the Swiss cantons, who had been sent by Switzerland to Utrecht to petition in favour of us, determined, in spite of his great age, to strike a last blow on our behalf. He left Utrecht for the north, obtained from Charles XII, King of Sweden, a letter of recommendation to the Queen of England, and others from the Kings of Denmark, and Prussia; from several German Protestant princes; from the States-General of the United Provinces; from the Swiss Protestant cantons; and from all the powers of the same religion. He then crossed the sea, and requested Lord Oxford (then prime minister of England) to procure him an audience. The minister asked the object of his mission.

'I have these letters,' said the marquis, 'to present to Her Majesty,' and named the correspondents.

'Give them to me,' said His Lordship, 'I will warmly back them up.'

'I cannot,' said the marquis, 'for I have strict orders from these powers to place them in Her Majesty's own hand, or bring them back.'

Upon this, Lord Oxford procured him the audience, and he presented the letters. The Queen promised to examine them, and give him an answer. For a fortnight he heard nothing. At the end of that period, knowing the Queen was going to walk in St James's Park, he went thither, and the Queen, having perceived him, ordered him to be called to her side, and said, 'Monsieur de Rochegude, I beg you to let those poor fellows on board the galleys of France know they will be released immediately.' As this pious and favourable answer had nothing doubtful in it, the marquis at once informed us by way of Geneva.

Soon after, an order came from the court to the governor at Marseilles to send up a list of all the Huguenots at the galleys; and then, at the end of May, a further order arrived to release one hundred and thirty-six; altogether there were three hundred of us. A list of names to be released was also sent.

The governor, having received this order, communicated it to the Missionaries, who were furious, saying that the King had been surprised and overreached, and that to release us would be an eternal blot upon the Catholic Church. They asked, prayed, that the governor suspend the execution of the order for a fortnight, that they might send an express to the court at Paris to get the order reversed. The governor, who refused these fathers nothing for fear of drawing down their hatred, granted their request, keeping the release order secret.

But, from the next day, we were informed, by degrees, of the list and the names on it. I was kept in great suspense, as I was the last mentioned, and did not hear for three days that my name was there at all – but imagine the feelings of affliction of those brethren whose names were not in the list. They comforted themselves, however, with the fact that Anne had asked for, and obtained, the release of us all. And that therefore their turn would come.

But then we learned the Missionaries had written to the court to obtain the reversal of the order, and knew by sad experience that these gentlemen were seldom refused. We could not sleep until the answer to the Missionaries' express arrived at last at Marseilles, which, to their great astonishment, brought no answer, good nor bad. This, judged the governor, meant the King wished his orders carried out. The Missionaries now sent off another express, demanding a further week. This arrived back with the same silence. At this they were quite confounded, and now asked the governor in what manner he was going to release us. The governor replied his orders were, 'Perfect liberty to go where they liked.' They strongly opposed this, maintaining that heretics like us, spreading themselves all over the kingdom, would pervert not only new converts, but even good Catholics. And then persuaded the governor to declare it a condition that we left the kingdom immediately by sea, never to return to it, on pain of being sent back to the galleys for life.

This was another instance of their cunning and malignance, for how could we leave by sea? There was not a ship in the harbour going to Holland or England, nor had we the means to engage one large enough to carry so many people. This the Missionaries foresaw, and were delighted that it seemed to leave us without any resource.

It is the custom, when slaves are to be released, to announce it to them some days before. One day, then, the argousin received an order from the governor to conduct the one hundred and thirty-six of us to the arsenal at Marseilles. There, having called us each by name, he declared that the King granted us our liberty on condition that we left the kingdom by sea at our own expense. We said that this was almost impossible for us to effect.

'That is your affair,' said he, 'The King is not going to spend a sou on you.'

'That being the case,' said we, 'order, sir, if you please, that we may be allowed to seek for some way of leaving by sea.'

'That is only fair,' said he, and gave orders to the argousins to allow us to go along the harbour with a guard, to look for a passage, as often, and wherever we liked. Now the Missionaries declared we must state where we wished to go. Their design was this: they knew we all had relations out of the kingdom: in Holland, in England, in Switzerland. They thought that he who said 'Holland', would be told to wait till there was a Dutch ship, and the same with England, and to those who said 'Switzerland', they would be told that they must be taken to Italy, but expected these latter would be in the minority.

Knowing nothing about this, we were again summoned to the arsenal and ascended a gallery, at the end of which was the office of the commissary of the navy, sitting there with the reverend fathers. This gallery being long and narrow, we were obliged to stand in single file, waiting to hear what they had to announce. He who was at the head of the list had his relations at Geneva; and being asked where he wished to go, said, 'To Geneva.' He who stood behind him, thought that all of us were to say the same, 'To Geneva.' So, turning to the one behind him, he said, 'Pass the word: "To Geneva."' This was done. For the commissary having heard several answer 'To Geneva,' said, 'I think they all want to go to Geneva.'

'Yes, sir,' we all replied, 'to Geneva.' Of course, as we could not go from Marseilles to Geneva by sea, and could not pass through France, we needed to find vessels to take us to Italy, a great detour. However, us all saying 'To Geneva,' facilitated our deliverance, as will be seen.

We were searching, seemingly in vain, for a boat to

take us to Italy, when a pilot of the galley *La Favorite*, named Jovas, told one of our brethren that he had a tartane, a kind of Mediterranean bark, in which he would willingly convey us from Marseilles to Villafranca, a seaport in the county of Nice, belonging to the King of Sardinia, and consequently out of France, from whence we might reach Geneva through Piedmont. We were delighted to have found this opportunity and quickly made a bargain with Captain Jovas: six francs a head for passage and food. He was also much pleased, as it was a profitable freight, Villafranca being only sixty to seventy-five miles from Marseilles. One of our brethren, and Captain Jovas, went to inform the governor of the arrangements. The governor expressed himself content; and would at once prepare our passports.

But when the Missionaries heard, they went at once to the governor; and said that the town was too near the frontiers of France, and that we should creep back across the border again, although they well knew that once out of France, nothing could make us return, bleeding, as we still were, with the wounds we had received there.

'No!' they said, we must be transported to Genoa, Leghorn, or Oneglia. This was pure malice for they knew that the journey from Villafranca to Geneva was much shorter than from Genoa or Leghorn. Besides, from these latter places, we should have to cross the Alps, an impossibility with our decrepit old men, paralytics, and cripples.

The governor, as well as every one else, saw it was only a cunning pretext to inflict on us more torment, but as he, like everyone else, was obliged to bend to their will, we were told that the agreement we had made with Captain Jovas could not be carried out, Villafranca being too close to France. Now Captain Jovas, furious with the Missionaries from spite, or kindness to us – or probably for his own profit – told us our bargain with him still held good, and he would still take us for six francs a head, even if it were to the other side of the world.

The governor was delighted, telling the Missionaries he was already risking his head in not executing the King's precise orders, and if the Queen of England complained, it might fare very ill with him, then ordered our immediate release. The Missionaries retaliated by telling the governor that Jovas' tartane was too small to carry one hundred and thirty-six men in its hold, and that he would be obliged to allow the greater number of us to travel on deck, and being desperate criminals, we would mutiny and throw Jovas and his crew into the sea, to sail whither we please. They could not give their consent to the souls and bodies of Jovas and his men being exposed to such an evident danger. In a word, they wanted us in vessels where we could be confined in their holds.

The governor saw the absurdity of this, but dared not resist it; so new orders were issued to provide ourselves with vessels capable of confining us all in the hold.

Jovas, further enraged, now poured forth against them (in secret, of course) a thousand imprecations, and swore he would get us to Italy, even if he lost by it, and next day, at his own expense, hired a further two barks, each of these taking fifty men in the hold, while his own would carry thirty-six. Again we went to the governor, who, to remove all pretext for delay, sent his secretary to examine the three tartanes, to assure him that they could take us all as Jovis maintained. We compounded with this official, for a favourable report, and it was agreed with the governor that the thirty-six which Captain Jovas were to take in his tartane should be released in two days, 17 June 1713, and that the other two barks should be dispatched at intervals of three days, each containing fifty more of us.

The Missionaries, near the end of their stratagems, now endeavoured to frighten the captains of the other two vessels, obliging them to sign a declaration not to land us at Villafranca, but at Oneglia, Leghorn, or Genoa, under penalty of a fine of four hundred francs, and the confiscation of their ships. Father Garcin, filled with spite and disappointment, left Marseilles that he might not behold the sight of our deliverance. On 17 June, the thirty-six men for Jovas' bark, of whom I was one, were brought to the arsenal where the commissary of the navy read us the King's orders, a copy of which were inserted in each of our passports. This done, the commissary ordered an argousin to unchain us completely, and giving our passports to Captain Jovas, told him that he gave our persons into his charge, and that he might start with us as soon as possible.

I left the arsenal free from my chains for the first time in thirteen years, and like a flock of lambs, we followed our captain, who led us to his bark, moored at the quay. We were about to go on board, and to descend into the hold, but the wind being contrary, and the sea very stormy, it was impossible to set sail.

Captain Jovas, seeing that we were resolutely about to enter his boat, to be shut up there, according to the will of the Missionaries, said to us, 'Do you think, gentlemen, I am as cruel as the Missionaries, and would keep you locked in the hold? No, I'm a seaman, and will use you as such. It is true,' he continued, 'we cannot leave harbour till the wind changes, but as the Lord knows when that will be, go into the city, and lodge at your ease. I do not fear your escaping, knowing that it would be more of a misfortune to be left behind. Just be sure to observe the weather, and when you see the wind change, return.' How strongly did the bluntness of this ignorant sailor contrast with the malicious civilities of our book-learned Missionaries.

We took his advice, and dispersed ourselves among different inns in the city. But no lodging, however comfortable, could diminish our dread of some new machination of the Jesuits. Therefore, the next morning, we waited upon the commissary to inform him of the reasons of our delay, that of the weather.

He, in return, simply said with a good natured air, 'The King, sirs, has not given you freedom in order for you to perish at sea. Stay in town till the wind becomes favourable, only permit me to advise you not to go out of the gates. Otherwise I wish you a hearty and prosperous voyage.'

After three days, the wind changed, but it still continued stormy. We went, notwithstanding, to the bark, where we found Captain Jovas, and asked to be put on board.

'Gentlemen,' says he, 'it is true we can now leave harbour, but you will find it terrible at sea.' We entreated him to risk it, telling him we had rather be in the hands of God than of man.

'I understand,' replied he, 'Come then, let's embark.'

We took in some provisions and left, but might have been better taking his advice, as the sea was most violent, and the waves so high that we were all soon seasick, and quite dispirited. The ship, too, was damaged, and Jovas was obliged to cast anchor before Toulon, about thirty miles from Marseilles, to repair some tackle. Here, about five in the evening, a sergeant and two soldiers belonging to the marine of Toulon boarded our vessel to summon Jovas to go before the governor of that city, to account for himself. We trembled with fear, reflecting that it was specified on our passports that we were to leave the kingdom, without ever returning, under penalty of being sent for life to the galleys. We dreaded we might find a governor who was ill-disposed, and who therefore might arrest us provisionally, and if he made this known to the Missionaries, they could easily accuse us of disobedience to the King's orders, and bring us once more into danger and trouble.

Jovas was equally vexed. However, he took our passports and got into the soldiers' boat to go and speak to the governor, permitting four of us, of whom I was one, to accompany him. As we were rowing into the harbour, a thought struck me, which, by God's grace, was very helpful to us. At that time the plague was raging in the Levant, so they took the precaution of furnishing all those who left Marseilles, either by sea or land, with a bill of health. The clerk of the office, who had given us our bill of health, had not enough room on it for all our names, but had written as an abridgement: 'Allow thirty-six men to pass, who are going to Italy by the King's orders, and who are in good health.' I suggested to Captain Jovas, that showing this form to the governor might be enough.

The five of us being brought before the governor, Jovas was asked to explain his journey and cargo. He replied, 'My cargo, sir, consists of thirty-six men, and here is their destination.' He then handed over the bill of health mentioning the 'King's orders'. The governor at once imagined that it was a secret expedition of the court, the object of which was no business of his. He told the captain he did not wish to know anything more; and that we might lodge in the town as long as we liked at his expense. We thanked him, and retired much pleased. We then begged Captain Jovas to land our companions, that they, too, might refresh themselves after the sickness they had suffered in the bark. This he did, and next morning, quite early, we all re-embarked and continued our voyage.

After three days we arrived off Villafranca, which town, as I have said, belongs to the King of Sardinia. Having anchored, we asked our captain to allow us ashore to sleep for the night, to come on board again next morning.

'I will willingly, gentlemen,' said he, 'do you this pleasure. But hope you will not abuse my kindness, for, being once in the town, you are your own masters, and need not embark again. But if you play me that trick, you will place me in the greatest embarrassment, for you know the declaration I have signed, not to land you at this port.' We gave him our word, and without the least scruple he at once put us on shore; where we lodged in four or five inns close to the port.

Next day, which was Sunday, we were preparing to re-embark when Jovas told us that he had to go and see someone at Nice, about three miles way. That he should also attend Mass there, and that when he returned he would take us back on board. I asked if he would allow me to go with him to see the town of Nice.

'Willingly,' replied he; and three of my brethren joining me, we all five went thither. On entering Nice, the captain went off to Mass, saying we should wait for him in the first inn we saw. We did so, and on his return we all walked through a long street, where, as it was Sunday and all the shops and houses shut, we saw scarcely any one. A little man coming towards us, saluted us very civilly, and begged us not to take it in bad part if he asked whence we came.

'Marseilles,' I replied.

He did not dare ask if we came from the galleys, as this offers too great an insult to a man, but instead said, 'I beg you, gentlemen, to tell me if you left by the King's order?'

'Yes, sir,' we replied, 'from the galleys of France.'

'Gracious God!' he exclaimed, 'You are those who were released a few days ago?'

We avowed we were. This man, quite transported with joy, asked us to follow him. We did so without hesitation, accompanied by our captain, who was afraid of some snare for us, for he did not trust Italians. We were led to the man's house, more like the palace of a great nobleman than that of a merchant. Having entered and closed the door, he embraced us with tears of joy, and calling his wife and children, said, 'See! Our dear brethren! Come out of the great tribulation of the galleys of France.'

All embraced us, praising God. After which, M

Bonijoli (this was his name) begged us to join him in prayers. We all knelt, Captain Jovas as well, and M Bonijoli offered up a prayer on the subject of our deliverance, which melted us to tears. After prayers, as they were getting breakfast ready, M Bonijoli asked us how many had been released. We told him thirty-six.

'That agrees with my letter,' said he 'Where are the others?'

'At Villafranca,' said we. We told him our story, and by what chance we found ourselves at Nice.

'But in your turn, sir,' said we, 'let us know who you are, and by what chance it was that you met us in the street.'

'I am,' said he, 'from Nîmes, in Languedoc. I left after the Revocation of the Edict, and, under the protection of the King of Sardinia, established myself in this town, where, by God's blessing, I have prospered. And though myself and my family are the only Protestants, we live in perfect tranquillity as regards religion, as our sovereign here will not suffer any of his subjects, either lay or ecclesiastical, to trouble me. In reply to your other question, I must tell you that one of my correspondents at Marseilles wrote to me on the day of your release, and begged me, if by chance you should pass through this town, to assist you. As for our meeting this morning in the street, I am sure it was Divine Providence causing me to go out of my house, which I never do on Sundays.'

Having mutually edified each other, by admiring the secret ways in which God manifests his power, we discussed the best plan of continuing our journey to Geneva, Captain Jovas producing the copy of the declaration which he had signed at Marseilles, forbidding him to land us at Villafranca. That he had to call at Villafranca was not difficult to justify, under the pretext of bad weather, a great excuse for all navigators; still, not to continue his voyage onwards to Oneglia, Leghorn, or Genoa, would be a manifest contravention of his orders. We could, of course, simply refuse to sail, but honour and our conscience opposed such an act.

On the other hand, M Bonijoli pointed out that if we landed at any of Oneglia, Leghorn, or Genoa, we should have almost insurmountable troubles reaching Geneva on account of the mountains; added to which we would not find horses or mules for so large a company, except at exorbitant prices. The only other thing would be to hire a vessel to take us to Holland or England, but this would be far too expensive for us. What, then, was to be done? We sat looking at each other – when suddenly M Bonijoli exclaimed that he might have a solution. At the Peace of Utrecht, he said, the King of France had restored the town and county of Nice to the Duke of Savoy, but after the French evacuation he left at Nice a commissary, there to regulate matters of debt, etc., which were in dispute between the court of France and that of Turin. The name of this French commissary was M Carboneau. He was on very friendly terms with M Bonijoli, and their children were of an age, so that the commissary had become quite at home in Bonijoli's house.

And it was in connection with this commissary that M Bonijoli framed his project. He begged Captain Jovas to give him a copy of his agreement, which he willingly did, and then that we wait a little, whilst he went out. An hour after he returned, accompanied by M Carboneau, the French commissary. The commissary questioned Jovas with an air of authority that his office gave him. Where was Jovas going? Why? What was his cargo? Hearing Jovas' replies, M Carboneau ordered him, in the name of the King of France, to land the rest of his thirty-six men, and to bring them to Nice, forbidding him, under penalty of disobedience to the King, from leaving the harbour of Villafranca with his bark, except by his, M Carboneau's, orders. Captain Jovas submitted, sailed back to Villafranca immediately, and brought back the remainder of our brethren, whom M Bonijoli lodged at various inns, at his own expense.

We four he kept in his own house, giving us the best cheer possible, the three days we remained in the town, these being employed in satisfying the vanity of the commissary who made us come every morning before his house, when, standing on the balcony in a dressing gown with a list of our names, he would called us one after the other, with his air of authority, and manners of a fop, making us laugh in our sleeves as he enquired whence we came, the names of our parents, our ages, and other similar useless questions. All to show off his little authority to a crowd of citizens of the town, who assembled before his house to see what was going on. M Bonijoli had told us beforehand that the commissary was very conceited, and he exhorted us, as the best policy, to submit, out of the hope that he would aid us in continuing our journey from Nice to Geneva. On the third day of this performance, amply satisfied with his own importance, this commissary sent for Jovas, and placed a paper in his hand, which he told him to read.

This very authentic looking document, honoured with the printed arms of the King, and bearing in large letters 'On behalf of the King' said that he, commissary and director for His Most Christian Majesty, having learned that a French bark had entered into the port of Villafranca, which had been chased and pursued to the entrance of the said port by two Neapolitan corsairs, he had gone to Villafranca, and had found that this bark was from Marseilles, and contained thirty-six men delivered from the galleys of France, bound for Italy. Having examined the men he had found them destitute. That, moreover, as the Neapolitan corsairs were waiting out at sea, in sight of Villafranca, to seize the said bark, he, the commissary, always attentive to the interests of the French nation, had, in the King's name, ordered the captain of this bark, named Jovas, to land these thirty-six men, that they might, from thence, make their journey to Geneva, which was their destination. And that, notwithstanding the protestation which the said Captain Jovis had made, in virtue of an agreement which he had signed at Marseilles, engaging, under heavy penalties, not to land them at Villafranca, he, the commissary, had forced him to do so, in virtue of the authority which His Majesty had confided to him in the county of Nice, etc., etc. Having given this declaration to Jovas, he asked him if he was content with it.

'Quite content, sir,' replied the captain.

'Very well,' replied the commissary, 'Set sail for Marseilles whenever you like, and throw any blame which they try to impute to you on me, saying I forced you to obey.'

Captain Jovas was well satisfied. Being now released from a much longer voyage, and his money, which we paid him at once, easily gained. He left for Marseilles, promising to inform the two other barks, which he would meet on his way, to come to Villafranca to receive the same treatment from this kind commissary. Thus all one hundred and thirty-six of us landed at this port, and journeyed then to Geneva on mules generously provided by that good man, M Bonijoli.

Initially hiring thirty-six mules and a guide to take our party as far as Turin, we left Nice at the beginning of July. Although we had much trouble from the more elderly, they scarcely being able to ride, we eventually crossed those frightful mountains, the summit of which, called the Col di Tenda, is so high that it always seems in the clouds. And though it was the height of summer, here we suffered such cold that we were obliged to descend from our mules and walk, in order to warm ourselves. Lofty and steep as this mountain is, there is no difficulty in ascending it, for a convenient road has been made in zigzags to the top.

We descended on the other side into the plain of Piedmont, the most beautiful and agreeable country in the world, and eventually arrived at Turin, its capital. We lodged at different inns, and the next morning received the visits of several French Huguenots, of whom a great number reside in the city. These gentlemen received us with zeal and cordiality, defraying all our expenses during the three days which we remained in this great city. After which, having found us new mules, they petitioned the King of Sardinia to give us a passport to traverse his states as far as Geneva. His Majesty, Victor Amadeus, wished to see us, and six of us were admitted to an audience where the ambassadors of Holland and England were also present. We were given a favourable reception, and His Majesty questioned us for half an hour about the galleys, and the sufferings we had endured. We were then asked if we had money for our journey. We replied not much, but that our brethren, especially M Bonijoli, of Nice, had had the charity to defray our expenses as far as Turin, and that our brethren here at Turin were preparing to do the same as far as Geneva.

His Majesty said upon this, 'Remain in Turin as long as you please, and when you want to leave, come to the office of my secretary of state, and take a passport I will order made ready.' We said, with his permission, we would like to start on the morrow.

'Go, then, under God's protection,' said this prince. He then ordered his secretary to immediately prepare a passport, not only giving permission to pass through his states, but ordered all his subjects to afford us help and succour during our journey.

There was at Turin a young man, a watchmaker by trade, belonging to Geneva, who, wanting to go home, asked to accompany us. About two days journey from Geneva, he took leave of us, saying that he knew a path which would give him a shorter route, but which our mules could not follow. We wished him a prosperous journey. Arriving at Geneva a day before us, he related our story, and that we were to arrive the next day.

That same next day, a Sunday, we arrived at a small village on a hill, about a league from Geneva, which we observed with a joy which can only be compared to the Israelites sighting of Canaan. We wished to go down immediately, but our guide told us that the gates of Geneva were never opened on Sunday until after divine service, that is, about four in the afternoon. We remained in the village till that time, then began to descend. At about half a mile from the town we perceived three carriages coming to meet us, surrounded by soldiers, and an immense crowd of people of both sexes and all ages. A servant approached and begged us to alight, that we might salute with decorum their excellencies of Geneva, who had come to welcome us.

We obeyed, and from each of the three carriages a magistrate and a minister descended, who embraced us with tears of joy, and praises for our constancy and resignation, praises far surpassing anything we deserved. We, in turn, praised and magnified God, who alone had sustained us. Then the people were given permission to approach: the most touching spectacle that can be imagined, as several had relations at the galleys, and wished to know whether those for whom they had sighed for so many years were amongst us. 'My son! My husband! My brother! Are you there?' Imagine the embraces given to those of our party who were recognised!

After, their excellencies ordered us to mount again, to make our entry into the town, which we did with the greatest difficulty, not being able to tear ourselves from the arms of our zealous brethren, who seemed to fear to lose sight of us. They had just constructed at Geneva a magnificent building, in which to lodge and board those citizens who had fallen into want. Though completed and furnished, it was, as yet, empty. Their excellencies suggested dedicating it by lodging us there. They led us thither, and we alighted in a spacious courtyard. Those who had relatives among our party, entreated their excellencies to allow them to take them home, which was willingly granted.

M Bousquet, one of us, had his mother and two sisters come to claim him. As he was my intimate friend, he begged their excellencies to permit me to go with him. And, following this example, all the citizens entreated to be allowed the consolation of lodging a brother in their houses, so that not one of us remained to lodge in the building. As to myself, I did not stay long at Geneva, for, with six of our brethren, I found a coach which had brought to Geneva the chargé d'affaires of the King of Prussia. As this was returning empty, we made a bargain with the coachman to take us as far as Frankfurt am Main. The gentlemen of Geneva kindly paid for this carriage, and money for expenses.

We seven, therefore, left Geneva, and arrived at Frankfurt in good health at the beginning of August. Here our friends in Geneva had recommended us to M Sarazin, a merchant, and elder of the Reformed Church at Bockenheim, about three miles from Frankfurt. He and his consistory, French as well as German, were assembled there and received us with joy, and strongly urged us to remain some days at Frankfurt, but we begged them to be allowed to continue to Holland. M Sarazin undertook to arrange our departure and pay our expenses, and bought for us a light boat, covered with a tent, with two men to row and steer as far as Cologne. He furnished us with provisions, and ordered the boatmen to land us every evening at convenient and comfortable places, where we might sleep and refresh ourselves, and especially to keep as near as possible to the German side, where the Emperor's army was encamped. For we much feared falling into the hands of the French army, which was then besieging Landau, being on the other side of the river.

M Sarazin, before we embarked, took us to the *hôtel de ville* to ask the magistrates to give us a passport. These gentlemen, all Lutherans, congratulated us upon our deliverance, and gave us a passport for which they charged us nothing. Our voyage to Cologne was a long one, a week, because always keeping close to the German bank, we had to stop at each fort and picket to show our passport. But once there we sold our boat, and the next day we left for Dordrecht. We made no stay there, but started at once for Rotterdam, where we were welcomed with every possible kindness by the numerous flock of our fellow-Protestants, French as well as Dutch, and after two days proceeded to Amsterdam, the termination of our long journey.

It would be impossible to describe the reception given to us in that great city. We went in a body to the venerable company of the consistory of the Walloon Church, to testify our gratitude to them for the constant kindnesses which they had shown during so many years, by helping us so efficaciously in our great tribulation, and then remained wandering from place to place for three or four weeks, not knowing where to settle ourselves, so affectionately were we everywhere received.

I was beginning to think how I could now usefully employ myself, when the consistory of the Walloon Church begged me to be one of the deputies to be sent to England for two objects. One to thank Her Britannic Majesty for the deliverance which she had obtained for us; the other to solicit Her Majesty to obtain the release of those who still remained at the galleys, about another two hundred people. I set out, then, for London with twelve deputies, all liberated galley slaves.

The Marquis de Miremont[38] and the Marquis de Rochegude presented us to the Queen, and de Miremont gave a short but very pathetic harangue, praising her in having been able to obtain the deliverance of the galley slaves. Her Majesty assured us she was very glad at our deliverance, and hoped soon to be able to release those who still remained at the galleys. The Marquis de Rochegude then judged it fitting to present us to the Duc d'Aumont,[39] then ambassador of the King of France, thinking this might be a useful step. Wishing to make this ambassador himself desire to see us, de Rochegude told him we were a deputation of Protestant galley slaves, whom Her Most Christian Majesty, together with the King of France, had released, and who had now come to London to thank the Queen, and who would have come to offer their respects to His Excellency if they had dared.

The ambassador, being curious to see us, settled that the marquis should introduce us on the morrow. At that audience we were received very graciously, he shaking hands with us, and congratulating us on our release. He asked us how long we had suffered, and the occasion of our sentences. Each replied to this question separately, for the time and occasion of each were different. We then heartily thanked the French King, in the person of his ambassador, beseeching him to deliver those who still remained captives. His Excellency said he could not understand why there were still some who had not been released, unless they had committed some other crime. We protested to the contrary, and I took the liberty of asking the ambassador to give me his attention for a moment, that I might prove that it was no difference in crimes which kept our brethren in the galleys.

I told him succinctly, the story of Daniel Le Gras, and myself; how we had both been condemned by the same sentence to the galleys for life, our two names on the one paper, yet I was released while Daniel remained, which very clearly proved that the court of France had not released the one hundred and thirty-six on any account of difference in their crimes. The ambassador, appearing convinced by this example, begged me to write it down. He said he thought that the minister of marine, and his secretaries, had made this blunder and assured the Marquis de Rochegude that he would write to the French court.

'And in proof I speak sincerely,' said he to M de Rochegude, 'come tomorrow, which is the post-day for France, and I will read and seal in your presence the letter.' Turning to his secretary, the abbé Nadal, he said, 'Here, monsieur l'abbé, are honest men, who, notwithstanding their religious prejudices, show much candour and good faith.' The abbé replied by a slight inclination of the head, but afterwards showed that the kindnesses with which his master honoured us were not to his taste. For next day, the Marquis de Rochegude having gone to the ambassador to inspect the letter, His Excellency, after receiving him in the most gracious manner, called the abbé Nadal, asking for the letter.

'Letter, my lord?' said the abbé.

'The letter,' said the ambassador, 'on the subject of the confessors at the galleys.' This honourable title of confessors, which His Excellency gave us, made the abbé shudder, as he coldly replied that it was upon His Excellency's desk.

'Give it me, then,' said the ambassador.

Thereupon the abbé told him that he wished a word in private; and having whispered in his ear, the ambassador then told the marquis that his abbé had reminded him that he had also enclosed in the letter some private matters, which did not concern the galley slaves, and that, therefore, he begged to dispense with showing it, but that he might be assured it should be sent that very day. M de Rochegude saw that the abbé had dissuaded his master from sending the letter, and though the ambassador continually assured M de Rochegude that the letter had been sent, neither he nor we believed it, and our brethren were not released for a year after, and then by a new solicitation from the Queen of England. I have described this incident to show that honest people pitied us, and were inclined to render us service, and that it was only the ecclesiastics who hated us.

This abbé Nadal was both chaplain and secretary to the embassy, and during his residence in London gave several proofs of his animosity against the Huguenots. He had so gained over the officers of the household, and so strongly incited them against the French refugees, that these gentlemen became so bold as to annoy our people even in their churches. For one Sunday morning, when the minister, Armand du Bordieu, was preaching at the Great Savoy (as the principal French church is called), one of these officials cried out, quite loud, 'You lie!' And then quickly escaped; for this insolence so excited the people that they would have torn him in pieces if they could.

Another time I witnessed an officer of the French embassy, at a cafe near the Exchange, saying that the refugees ought to be hanged. Someone represented that he ought to be more circumspect, since, by God's grace, they were now in a land of liberty.

The insolent reply, was, 'Do you think, gentlemen, the

King of France has not arms long enough to reach you beyond the sea? I hope that you will soon find it so,' at which a London merchant, M Banal, a good refugee, became so excited he gave this officer one of the most violent boxes on the ear which I have ever seen, saying, 'This arm, though perhaps not so long as that of your King's, now reaches you from a nearer place.'

The officer put his hand to his sword, but all the Frenchmen who were there fell upon him with a great many blows, and determined to throw him out of the window of the second storey, which would certainly have happened had not the mistress of the cafe besought, with clasped hands, that he might be allowed to go out at the door, which was allowed out of consideration for the woman, but not without a further good thrashing. He ran to carry his complaint to the ambassador, who, far from justifying him, said that not only had he deserved what he got, but deserved a second punishment from the King, in that he could not understand how an officer of the King could insult anybody. These incidents truly show of what the Jesuits and their allies are capable. If they seek to persecute in the safest of asylums, one may judge of what happens to those in their power.

I shall finish, as I have promised, my memoirs with the year 1713. Having resided in London for about two months and a half, and having nothing more to detain me there, I left in the month of December. I arrived back at The Hague, where I communicated what had happened in London, not forgetting the praise which an immense number of persons, Englishmen as well as French refugees, deserved. For, besides different presents from private individuals, the consistory of the Savoy church defrayed our expenses during our sojourn in London.

I stayed nine weeks at The Hague where the minister, M Basnage, presented me to several noblemen, who wished to obtain a pension for us, which Their Highnesses granted. I felt that we in no way deserved this benevolence, and cherish a gratitude beyond all expression for it. May God be the rewarder of their virtues, and to the end of time may he richly bestow upon their republic his most gracious blessings!

Notes

1. Curry, E. Hamilton, *The Man-of-War* (London & Edinburgh: T. C. & E. C. Jack, n.d.), p.21.
2. Ward et al, (eds), *The Cambridge History of English and American Literature: an encyclopedia in eighteen volumes* (London and New York, 1907-21), *Vol X: The Age of Johnson*, ix.
3. Fenwick, Kenneth, (ed) *Galley Slave: The Autobiography of Jean Marteilhe* (London: Folio Society, 1957), x.
4. Translator's preface, Religious Tract Society edition (n.d. [c. 1880]), ix.
5. Evelyn, John, *Diaries*, Vol II, ed. William Beat (London: Henry Colburn, 1850), accessed via University of California Libraries http://www.archive.org/details/diarycorrespondeo2eveliala.
6. Quoted in translator's preface, Religious Tract Society edition (n.d. [c. 1880]), xi-xii.
7. Ezekiel, 27:5-9.
8. Sanders, Thomas, *A most lamentable Voyage made into Turkey* (London: Stationers Hall, 1584; Hakluyt, 1589), p.9.
9. Marteilhe, Jean, *Memoirs of a Protestant Condemned to the Galleys of France*, trans. James Willington [Oliver Goldsmith] (Dublin: Watts, 1765), p.211.
10. Bamford, Paul W., *Fighting Ships and Prisons: the Mediterranean Galleys of France in the Age of Louis XIV* (University of Minnesota Press, 1973), p.5.
11. Crooke, Jon, *La Reale of France*, www.bigscalemodels.com/ships/lereale/lereale.html
12. Ibid.
13. Lane-Poole, Stanley, & J. D. Jerrold Kelley, *The Barbary Corsairs* (London: Fisher Unwin and New York: Putnam, 1890), pp.300-301.
14. Weiss, Charles, *History of the French Protestant Refugees from the Revocation of the Edict of Nantes to the Present Time* (Blackwood, Edinburgh, 1854), p.863.
15. Bion, John, *An Account of the Torments the French Protestants Endure aboard the Galleys* (London: John Morphew, 1708), edited

and abridged by Vincent McInerney as *The Sufferings of the Protestants in the French Galleys* (2007, unpublished), p.4. All subsequent references to Bion refer to this version.

16. Curry, E. Hamilton, *The Man-of-War* (London & Edinburgh: T. C. & E. C. Jack, n.d.), pp.24-25.

17. Ibid.

18. Ibid.

19. Bion, p.21.

20. Marteilhe, Jean, *Memoirs of a Protestant Condemned to the Galleys of France*, trans James Willington [Oliver Goldsmith] (Dublin: Watts, 1765), p.211.

21. Bion, p.6.

22. Bion, p.8.

23. Probably Major-General John Hill (d.1735), who began his career as a page at the court of Queen Anne and then progressed in the army through the influence initially of his cousin, Sarah, Duchess of Marlborough, and then later by that of his sister Abigail, Lady Masham, who was close to the Queen.

24. Gozzi, Carlo, *Memoirs*, Vol I, trans. John Addington Symonds (London: Nimmo, 1890), pp.213-221.

25. As quoted in Hobsbawm, Eric J., *The Age of Extremes: The Short Twentieth Century, 1914-1991*, accessed via Wikiquote http://en.wikiquote.org/wiki/Primo_Levi.

26. Henri-Jacques de Caumont (1675-1726), Duke de La Force, member of the Académie Française and Finance Minister of France.

27. The Jesuits were members of the Society of Jesus, the largest male religious order in the Catholic Church, with the aim of evangelisation through missionary and educational work. They were founded by St Ignatius Loyola and six other students from the University of Paris (including St Frances Xavier) who met in the crypt of the Church of St Denis, Monmartre, in August 1534.

28. In the Book of Genesis God sends angels to destroy the cities of Sodom and Gomorrah for their wickedness, but intends to spare Lot and his family. The angels therefore command Lot, his wife, and their two daughters to flee, without turning back to look at the destruction but Lot's wife does look back and is changed into a pillar of salt: Genesis 13:10-13 and 19:1-26. Later, in Luke 17:32, Jesus simply says 'Remember Lot's wife' as a warning to Christians not to return to sin.

29. Note on French currency: the livre was the currency of France until 1795. Several different livres existed, some concurrently. It was established by Charlemagne (742-814) as a unit of account

equal to one pound of silver and subdivided into 20 sous each of
12 denier. Between 1360 and 1641, coins worth one livre tournois
(Tours pound) were minted and known as francs. The livre at the
time of its replacement by the franc was worth about £2.50. The
name franc persisted in common parlance for one livre tournois
but was not used on coins or paper money. Louis XIII (1601-1643)
stopped minting the franc in 1641, replacing it with coins based on
the silver écu and gold louis d'or. These both fluctuated in value,
with the écu varying between five and six livres tournois until 1726
when it was fixed at six livres. The gold louis d'or was equal to 24
livres, along with a half-louis coin (the demi-louis d'or) and a
two-louis coin (the double louis d'or), 12 and 48 livres respectively.
The pistole is the French name given to a Spanish coin that was
also given to the louis d'or. One pistole was worth approximately
ten livres, with one livre being worth one franc when the latter
were issued about 1641. The franc was in turn replaced by the louis
d'or. There has never officially been a French 'crown', but the
word was sometimes used for the écu.

30. The Prince-Bishopric of Liège was a state of the Holy Roman
Empire in what is now Belgium. It was headed by the Prince-
Bishop of Liège and its territory included most of the present
Belgian provinces of Liège and Limburg. The capital was Liège.
The bishopric was dissolved in 1795, when Liège was conquered
by France.

31. Louis Phélypeaux (1672-1725), Marquis de La Vrillière, succeeded
his father, Balthazar Phélypeaux, in 1700 as minister for the
'Reformed Religion', that is, with responsibility for Huguenots. In
1715, he eventually became acting head of the department of the
Maison du Roi and of the Navy ministry.

32. Modern Tournai, in what was French Flanders.

33. 'Huissier' can mean an usher, or a server of process to a court, an
official who can effect seizures and evictions. An English
equivalent might lie between a bailiff and sheriff's officer.

34. Jean-Baptiste Andrault Langeron (1677-1754), Marquis de
Maulévrier.

35. Philips van Almonde (1646-1711), Dutch lieutenant admiral who
served in his nation's maritime conflicts of the seventeenth and
early eighteenth centuries.

36. Jean Bart (1651-1702) was a commander in the French navy and
a privateer. The son of a humble fisherman, he rose to the rank of
admiral and was most successful in the Nine Years' War (1688-
1697).

37. Louis II Phélypeaux (1643-1727), Comte de Pontchartrain, and

Secretary of State for the French navy from 1690.

38. Armand de Bourbon (1655-1732), Marquis de Miremont, came to England on the Revocation of the Edict of Nantes, was appointed to the command of a regiment of dragoons by James II in 1688, was afterwards an ADC to King William, and British commissioner to the congress of Utrecht, 1712.

39. Louis d'Aumont of Rochebaron (1666-1723), Marquis de Villequier, then Duc d'Aumont.

SEAFARERS' VOICES

A new series of seafaring memoirs

The lives and practices of our seafaring forbears have receded into the distant past, remote but also of fascination to a generation to whom the sea is now an alien place. This new series, *Seafarers' Voices*, presents a set of abridged and highly readable first-hand accounts of maritime voyaging, which describe life at sea from different viewpoints – naval, mercantile, officer and lower deck, men and women – and cover the years 1700 to the 1900s, from the end of the Mediterranean galleys, through the classic age of sail to the coming of the steamship. Published in chronological order, these memoirs unveil the extraordinary and unfamiliar world of our seafaring ancestors and show how they adapted to the ever-demanding and ever-changing world of ships and the sea, both at war and at peace.

The first titles in the series

1. *Galley Slave*, by Jean Marteilhe

2. *A Privateer's Voyage Round the World*, by Captain George Shelvocke

3. *Slaver Captain*, John Newton

4. *Landsman Hay*, Robert Hay

For more details visit our website
www.seaforthpublishing.com